D0037562

THE RESPONSIBILITIES OF
THE NOVELIST

Photographed by Arnold Genthe

FRANK NORRIS

THE RESPONSIBILITIES
OF THE NOVELIST

AND OTHER LITERARY
ESSAYS

BY

FRANK NORRIS

HASKELL HOUSE PUBLISHERS Ltd.
Publishers of Scarce Scholarly Books
NEW YORK, N. Y. 10012
1969

First Published 1903

HASKELL HOUSE PUBLISHERS LTD.
Publishers of Scarce Scholarly Books
280 LAFAYETTE STREET
NEW YORK. N. Y. 10012

Library of Congress Catalog Card Number: 68-26364

Standard Book Number 8383-0269-6

Printed in the United States of America

CONTENTS

CONTENTS—*Continued*

THE RESPONSIBILITIES OF
THE NOVELIST

THE RESPONSIBILITIES OF
THE NOVELIST

IT is not here a question of the "unarrived,"
the "unpublished"; these are the care-free
irresponsibles whose hours are halcyon and
whose endeavours have all the lure, all the
recklessness of adventure. They are not recognized; they have made no standards for
themselves, and if they play the *saltimbanque*
and the charlatan nobody cares and nobody
(except themselves) is affected.

But the writers in question are the successful
ones who have made a public and to whom
some ten, twenty or a hundred thousand
people are pleased to listen. You may believe
if you choose that the novelist, of all workers,
is independent—that he can write what he
pleases, and that certainly, certainly he should
never "write down to his readers"—that he
should never consult them at all.

On the contrary, I believe it can be proved
that the successful novelist should be more
than all others limited in the nature and character of his work more than all others he should

3

be careful of what he says; more than all others he should defer to his audience; more than all others—more even than the minister and the editor—he should feel "his public" and watch his every word, testing carefully his every utterance, weighing with the most relentless precision his every statement; in a word, possess a sense of his responsibilities.

For the novel is the great expression of modern life. Each form of art has had its turn at reflecting and expressing its contemporaneous thought. Time was when the world looked to the architects of the castles and great cathedrals to truly reflect and embody its ideals. And the architects—serious, earnest men—produced such "expressions of contemporaneous thought" as the Castle of Coucy and the Church of Notre Dame. Then with other times came other customs, and the painters had their day. The men of the Renaissance trusted Angelo and Da Vinci and Velasquez to speak for them, and trusted not in vain. Next came the age of drama. Shakespeare and Marlowe found the value of x for the life and the times in which they lived. Later on contemporary life had been so modified that neither painting, architecture nor drama was the best vehicle of expression, the day of the longer poems arrived, and Pope and Dryden spoke for their fellows.

Thus the sequence   Each age speaks with its own peculiar organ, and has left the Word for us moderns to read and unders and.   The Castle of Coucy and the Church of Notre Dame are the spoken words of the Middle Ages.   The Renaissance speaks—and intelligib y—to us through the sibyls of the Sistine chapel and the Mona Lisa.   "Macbeth" and "Tamerlane" *résumé* the whole spirit of the Elizabethan age, while the "Rape of the Lock" is a wireless message to us straight from the period of the Restoration.

To-day is the day of the novel.   In no other day and by no other vehicle is contemporaneous life so adequately expressed; and the critics of the twenty-second century, reviewing our times, striving to reconstruct our civilization, will look not to the painters, not to the architects nor dramatists, but to the novelists to find our idiosyncrasy.

I think this is true.   I think if the matter could in any way be statisticized, the figures would bear out the assumption.   There is no doubt the novel will in time "go out" of popular favour as irrevocably as the long poem has gone, and for the reason that it is no longer the right mode of expression.

It is interesting to speculate upon what will take its place.   Certainly the coming civilization will revert to no former means of expressing its thought or its ideals. Possibly music will be the interpreter of the life of the twenty-first and twenty-second centuries. Possibly one may see a hint of this in the characterization of Wagner's operas as the "Music of the Future."

This, however, is parenthetical and beside the mark. Remains the fact that to-day is the day of the novel. By this one does not mean that the novel is merely popular. If the novel was not something more than a simple diversion, a means of whiling away a dull evening, a long railway journey, it would not, believe me, remain in favour another day.

If the novel, then, is popular, it is popular with a reason, a vital, inherent reason; that is to say, it is essential. Essential—to resume once more the proposition—because it expresses modern life better than architecture, better than painting, better than poetry, better than music. It is as necessary to the civilization of the twentieth century as the violin is necessary to Kubelik, as the piano is necessary to Paderewski, as the plane is necessary to the carpenter, the sledge to the blacksmith, the chisel to the mason. It is an instrument, a tool, a weapon, a vehicle. It is that thing which, in the hand of man, makes him civilized and no longer savage, because it gives him a power of durable, permanent expression. So much for the novel—the instrument.

Because it is so all-powerful to-day, the people turn to him who wields this instrument with every degree of confidence. They expect —and rightly—that results shall be commensurate with means. The unknown archer who grasps the bow of Ulysses may be expected by the multitude to send his shaft far and true. If he is not true nor strong he has no business with the bow. The people give heed to him only because he bears a great weapon. He himself knows before he shoots whether or no he is worthy.

It is all very well to jeer at the People and at the People's misunderstanding of the arts, but the fact is indisputable that no art that is not in the end understood by the People can live or ever did live a single generation. In the larger view, in the last analysis, the People pronounce the final judgment. The People, despised of the artist, hooted, caricatured and vilified, are after all, and in the main, the real seekers after Truth. Who is it, after all, whose interest is liveliest in any given work of art? It is not now a question of *esthetic* interest— that is, the artist's, the amateur's, the *cognoscente's*. It is a question of *vital* interest. Say what you will, Maggie Tulliver—for instance

—is far more a living being for Mrs. Jones across the street than she is for your sensitive, fastidious, keenly critical artist, litterateur, or critic. The People—Mrs. Jones and her neighbours—take the life history of these fictitious characters, these novels, to heart with a seriousness that the esthetic cult have no conception of. The cult consider them almost solely from their artistic sides. The People take them into their innermost lives. Nor do the People discriminate. Omnivorous readers as they are to-day, they make little distinction between Maggie Tulliver and the heroine of the last "popular novel." They do not stop to separate true from false; they do not care.

How necessary it becomes, then, for those who, by the simple art of writing, can invade the heart's heart of thousands, whose novels are received with such measureless earnestness —how necessary it becomes for those who wield such power to use it rightfully. Is it not expedient to act fairly? Is it not in Heaven's name essential that the People hear, not a lie, but the Truth?

If the novel were not one of the most important factors of modern life; if it were not the completest expression of our civilization; if its influence were not greater than all the pulpits, than all the newspapers between the oceans, it would not be so important that its message should be true.

But the novelist to-day is the one who reaches the greatest audience. Right or wrong, the People turn to him the moment he speaks, and what he says they believe.

For the Million, Life is a contracted affair, is bounded by the walls of the narrow channel of affairs in which their feet are set. They have no horizon. They look to-day as they never have looked before, as they never will look again, to the writer of fiction to give them an idea of life beyond their limits, and they believe him as they never have believed before and never will again.

This being so, is it not difficult to understand how certain of these successful writers of fiction —these favoured ones into whose hands the gods have placed the great bow of Ulysses—can look so frivolously upon their craft? It is not necessary to specify. One speaks of those whose public is measured by "one hundred and fifty thousand copies sold." We know them, and because the gods have blessed us with wits beyond our deserving we know their work is false. But what of the "hundred and fifty thousand" who are not discerning and who receive this falseness as Truth, who believe this topsy-turvy picture of Life beyond their horizons is real and vital and sane?

There is no gauge to measure the extent of this malignant influence. Public opinion is made no one can say how, by infinitesimal accretions, by a multitude of minutest elements. Lying novels, surely, surely in this day and age of indiscriminate reading, contribute to this more than all other influences of present-day activity.

The Pulpit, the Press and the Novel—these indisputably are the great moulders of public opinion and public morals to-day. But the Pulpit speaks but once a week; the Press is read with lightning haste and the morning news is waste-paper by noon. But the novel goes into the home to stay. It is read word for word; is talked about, discussed; its influence penetrates every chink and corner of the family.

Yet novelists are not found wanting who write for money. I do not think this is an unfounded accusation. I do not think it asking too much of credulity. This would not matter if they wrote the Truth But these gentlemen who are "in literature for their own pocket every time" have discovered that for the moment the People have confounded the Wrong with the Right, and prefer that which is a lie to that which is true. "Very well, then," say these gentlemen. "If they want a lie they shall have it;" and they give the People a lie in return for royalties.

The surprising thing about this is that you and I and all the rest of us do not consider this as disreputable—do not yet realize that the novelist has responsibilities. We condemn an editor who sells his editorial columns, and we revile the pulpit attainted of venality. But the venal novelist—he whose influence is greater than either the Press or Pulpit—*him* we greet with a wink and the tongue in the cheek.

This should not be so. Somewhere the protest should be raised, and those of us who see the practice of this fraud should bring home to ourselves the realization that the selling of one hundred and fifty thousand books is a serious business. The People have a right to the Truth as they have a right to life, liberty and the pursuit of happiness. It is *not* right that they be exploited and deceived with false views of life, false characters, false sentiment, false morality, false history, false philosophy, false emotions, false heroism, false notions of self-sacrifice, false views of religion, of duty, of conduct and of manners.

The man who can address an audience of one hundred and fifty thousand people who—unenlightened—*believe what he says*, has a heavy duty to perform, and tremendous responsibilities to shoulder; and he should address himself to his task not with the flippancy of a catch-penny juggler at the county fair, but with earnestness, with soberness, with a sense of his limitations, and with all the abiding sincerity that by the favour and mercy of the gods may be his.

THE TRUE REWARD OF THE NOVELIST

THE TRUE REWARD OF THE NOVELIST

NOT that one quarrels with the historical novel as such; not that one does not enjoy good fiction wherever found, and in whatever class. It is the method of attack of the latter-day copyists that one deplores—their attitude, the willingness of so very, very many of them to take off the hat to Fashion, and then hold the same hat for Fashion to drop pennies in.

Ah, but the man must be above the work or the work is worthless, and the man better off at some other work than that of producing fiction. The eye never once should wander to the gallery, but be always with single purpose turned *inward* upon the work, testing it and retesting it that it rings true

What one quarrels with is the perversion of a profession, the detestable trading upon another man's success. No one can find fault with those few good historical novels that started the fad. There was good workmanship in these, and honesty. But the copyists, the fakirs—they are not novelists at all, though they write novels that sell by the hundreds of

thousands. They are business men. They
find out—no, they allow *some one else* to find
out—what the public wants, and they give it
to the public cheap, and advertise it as a new
soap is advertised. Well, they make money;
and, if that is their aim—if they are content to
prostitute the good name of American literature
for a sliding scale of royalties—let's have done
with them. They have their reward. But the
lamentable result will be that these copyists
will in the end so prejudice the people against
an admirable school of fiction—the school of
Scott—that for years to come the tale of historic
times will be discredited and many a great
story remain unwritten, and many a man of
actual worth and real power hold back in the
ranks for very shame of treading where so
many fools have rushed in.

For the one idea of the fakir—the copyist—
and of the public which for the moment listens
to him, is Clothes, Clothes, Clothes, first, last
and always Clothes. Not Clothes only in the
sense of doublet and gown, but Clothes of
speech, Clothes of manner, Clothes of customs.
Hear them expatiate over the fashion of wear-
ing a cuff, over a trick of speech, over the architecture of a house, the archeology of armour
and the like. It is all well enough in its way,
but so easily dispensed with if there be flesh and

blood underneath. Veronese put the people of his "Marriage at Cana" into the clothes of his contemporaries. Is the picture any less a masterpiece?

Do these Little People know that Scott's archeology was about one thousand years "out" in Ivanhoe, and that to make a parallel we must conceive of a writer describing Richelieu—say—in small clothes and a top hat? But is it not *Richelieu* we want, and *Ivanhoe*, not their clothes, their armour? And in spite of his errors Scott gave us a real Ivanhoe. He got beneath the clothes of an epoch and got the heart of it, and the spirit of it (different essentially and vitally from ours or from every other, the spirit of feudalism); and he put forth a masterpiece.

The Little People so very precise in the matter of buttons and "bacinets" do not so. Take the clothes from the people of their Romances and one finds only wooden manikins. Take the clothes from the epoch of which they pretend to treat and what is there beneath? It is only the familiar, well-worn, well-thumbed nineteenth or twentieth century after all. As well have written of Michigan Avenue, Chicago, as "La Rue de la Harpe," "The Great North Road" or the "Appian Way."

It is a masquerade, the novel of the copyists;

and the people who applaud them—are they not the same who would hold persons in respect because of the finery of their bodies? A poor taste, a cheap one; the taste of serving-men, the literature of chambermaids.

To approach the same subject by a different radius: why must the historical novel of the copyist always be conceived of in the terms of Romance? Could not the formula of Realism be applied at least as well, not the Realism of mere externals (the copyists have that), but the Realism of motives and emotions? What would we not give for a picture of the fifteenth century as precise and perfect as one of Mr. James's novels? Even if that be impossible, the attempt, even though half-way successful, would be worth while, would be better than the wooden manikin in the tin-pot helmet and baggy hose. At least we should get some-where, even if no farther than Mr. Kingsley took us in "Hereward," or Mr. Blackmore in "Lorna Doone."

How about the business life and the student life, and the artizan life and the professional life, and above all, the home life of historic periods? Great Heavens! There was some-thing else sometimes than the soldier life. They were not always cutting and thrusting, not always night-riding, escaping, venturing, posing.

Or suppose that cut-and-thrust must be the order of the day, where is the "man behind," and the heart in the man and the spirit in the heart and the essential vital, elemental, all-important true life within the spirit? We are all Anglo-Saxons enough to enjoy the sight of a fight, would go a block or so out of the way to see one, or be a dollar or so out of pocket. But let it not be these jointed manikins worked with a thread. At least let it be Mr. Robert Fitzsimmons or Mr. James Jeffries.

Clothes, paraphernalia, panoply, pomp and circumstance, and the copyist's public and the poor bedeviled, ink-corroded hack of an over-driven, underpaid reviewer on an inland paper speak of the "vivid colouring" and "the fine picture of a bygone age"—it is easy to be vivid with a pot of vermilion at the elbow. Any one can scare a young dog with a false-face and a roaring voice, but to be vivid and use grays and browns, to scare the puppy with the lifted finger, that's something to the point.

The difficult thing is to get at the life immediately around you—the very life in which you move. No romance in it? No romance in *you*, poor fool. As much romance on Michigan Avenue as there is realism in King Arthur's court. It is as you choose to see it. The important thing to decide is, which formula is the best to help you grip the Real Life of this or any other age. Contemporaries always imagine that theirs is the prosaic age, and that chivalry and the picturesque died with their forbears. No doubt Merlin mourned for the old time of romance. Cervantes held that romance was dead. Yet most of the historical romances of the day are laid in Cervantes's time, or even after it.

Romance and Realism are constant qualities of every age, day and hour. They are here to-day. They existed in the time of Job. They will continue to exist till the end of time, not so much in things as in point of view of the people who see things.

The difficulty, then, is to get at the immediate life—immensely difficult, for you are not only close to the canvas, but are yourself part of the picture.

But the historic age is almost done to hand. Let almost any one shut himself in his closet with a history and Violet LeDuc's *Dictionaire du Mobilier* and, given a few months' time, he can evolve an historical novel of the kind called popular. He need not know men—just clothes and lingo, the "what-ho-without-there" gabble. But if he only chose he could find romance and adventure in Wall Street or Bond Street. But romance there does not wear the gay clothes and the showy accouterments, and to discover it—the real romance of it—means hard work and close study, not of books, but of people and actualities.

Not only this, but to know the life around you you must live—if not *among* people, then *in* people. You must be something more than a novelist if you can, something more than just a writer. There must be that nameless sixth sense or sensibility in you that great musicians have in common with great inventors and great scientists; the thing that does not enter into the work, but that is back of it; the thing that would make of you a good *man* as well as a good novelist; the thing that differentiates the mere business man from the financier (for it is possessed of the financier and poet alike—so only they be big enough).

It is not genius, for genius is a lax, loose term so flippantly used that its expressiveness is long since lost. It is more akin to sincerity. And there once more we halt upon the great word—sincerity, sincerity, and again sincerity. Let the writer attack his historical novel with sincerity and he cannot then do wrong. He will see then the man beneath the clothes, and the heart beneath both, and he will be so amazed at the wonder of that sight that he will forget the clothes. His public will be small, perhaps, but he will have the better reward of the knowledge of a thing well done. Royalties on editions of hundreds of thousands will not pay him more to his satisfaction than that. To make money is not the province of a novelist. If he is the right sort, he has other responsibilities, heavy ones. He of all men cannot think only of himself or for himself. And when the last page is written and the ink crusts on the pen-point and the hungry presses go clashing after another writer, the "new man" and the new fashion of the hour, he will think of the grim long grind of the years of his life that he has put behind him and of his work that he has built up volume by volume, sincere work, telling the truth as he saw it, independent of fashion and the gallery gods, holding to these with gripped hands and shut teeth—he will think of all this then, and he will be able to say: "I never truckled; I never took off the hat to Fashion and held it out for pennies. By God, I told them the truth. They liked it or they didn't like it. What had that to do with me? I told them the truth; I knew it for the truth then, and I know it for the truth now."

And that is his reward—the best that a man may know; the only one really worth the striving for.

THE NOVEL WITH A "PURPOSE"

THE NOVEL WITH A "PURPOSE"

AFTER years of indoctrination and expostulation on the part of the artists, the people who read appear at last to have grasped this one precept—"the novel must not preach," but "the purpose of the story must be subordinate to the story itself." It took a very long time for them to understand this, but once it became apparent they fastened upon it with a tenacity comparable only to the tenacity of the American schoolboy to the date "1492." "The novel must not preach," you hear them say.

As though it were possible to write a novel without a purpose, even if it is only the purpose to amuse. One is willing to admit that this savours a little of quibbling, for "purpose" and purpose to amuse are two different purposes. But every novel, even the most frivolous, must have some reason for the writing of it, and in that sense must have a "purpose."

Every novel must do one of three things— it must (1) tell something, (2) show something, or (3) prove something. Some novels do all three of these; some do only two; all must do at least one.

The ordinary novel merely tells something, elaborates a complication, devotes itself primarily to *things*. In this class comes the novel of adventure, such as "The Three Musketeers."

The second and better class of novel shows something, exposes the workings of a temperament, devotes itself primarily to the minds of human beings. In this class falls the novel of character, such as "Romola."

The third, and what we hold to be the best class, proves something, draws conclusions from a whole congeries of forces, social tendencies, race impulses, devotes itself not to a study of men but of man. In this class falls the novel with the purpose, such as "Les Miserables."

And the reason we decide upon this last as the highest form of the novel is because that, though setting a great purpose before it as its task, it nevertheless includes, and is forced to include, both the other classes. It must tell something, must narrate vigorous incidents and must show something, must penetrate deep into the motives and character of type-men, men who are composite pictures of a multitude of men. It must do this because of the nature of its subject, for it deals with elemental forces, motives that stir whole nations. These cannot be handled as abstractions in fiction. Fiction can find expression only in the concrete. The elemental forces, then, contribute to the novel with a purpose to provide it with vigorous action. In the novel, force can be expressed in no other way. The social tendencies must be expressed by means of analysis of the characters of the men and women who compose that society, and the two must be combined and manipulated to evolve the purpose—to find the value of x.

The production of such a novel is probably the most arduous task that the writer of fiction can undertake. Nowhere else is success more difficult; nowhere else is failure so easy. Unskilfully treated, the story may dwindle down and degenerate into mere special pleading, and the novelist become a polemicist, a pamphleteer, forgetting that, although his first consideration is to prove his case, his *means* must be living human beings, not statistics, and that his tools are not figures, but pictures from life as he sees it. The novel with a purpose *is*, one contends, a preaching novel. But it preaches by telling things and showing things. Only, the author selects from the great storehouse of actual life the things to be told and the things to be shown, which shall bear upon his problem, his purpose. The preaching, the moralizing, is the result not of direct appeal by the writer, but is made—should be made—to the reader by the very incidents of the story.

But here is presented a strange anomaly, a distinction as subtle as it is vital. Just now one has said that in the composition of the kind of novel under consideration the *purpose* is for the novelist the all-important thing, and yet it is impossible to deny that the *story*, as a mere story, is to the story-writer the one great object of attention. How reconcile then these two apparent contradictions?

For the novelist, the purpose of his novel, the problem he is to solve, is to his story what the keynote is to the sonata. Though the musician cannot exaggerate the importance of the keynote, yet the thing that interests him is the sonata itself. The keynote simply coördinates the music, systematizes it, brings all the myriad little rebellious notes under a single harmonious code.

Thus, too, the purpose in the novel. It is important as an end and also as an ever-present guide. For the writer it is as important only as a note to which his work must be attuned. The moment, however, that the writer becomes really and vitally interested in his purpose his novel fails.

Here is the strange anomaly. Let us suppose

that Hardy, say, should be engaged upon a story which had for purpose to show the injustices under which the miners of Wales were suffering. It is conceivable that he could write a story that would make the blood boil with indignation. But he himself, if he is to remain an artist, if he is to write his novel successfully, will, as a novelist, care very little about the iniquitous labour system of the Welsh coal-mines. It will be to him as impersonal a thing as the key is to the composer of a sonata. As a man Hardy may or may not be vitally concerned in the Welsh coal-miner. That is quite unessential. But as a novelist, as an artist, his sufferings must be for him a matter of the mildest interest. They are important, for they constitute his keynote. They are *not* interesting for the reason that the working out of his *story*, its people, episodes, scenes and pictures, is for the moment the most interesting thing in all the world to him, exclusive of everything else. Do you think that Mrs. Stowe was more interested in the slave question than she was in the writing of "Uncle Tom's Cabin"? Her book, her manuscript, the page-to-page progress of the narrative, were more absorbing to her than all the Negroes that were ever whipped or sold. Had it not been so, that great purpose-novel never would have succeeded.

Consider the reverse—"Fecondité," for instance. The purpose for which Zola wrote the book ran away with him. He really did care more for the depopulation of France than he did for his novel. Result—sermons on the fruitfulness of women, special pleading, a farrago of dry, dull incidents, overburdened and collapsing under the weight of a theme that should have intruded only indirectly.

This is preëminently a selfish view of the question, but it is assuredly the only correct one. It must be remembered that the artist has a double personality, himself as a man, and himself as an artist. But, it will be urged, how account for the artist's sympathy in his fictitious characters, his emotion, the actual tears he sheds in telling of their griefs, their deaths, and the like?

The answer is obvious. As an artist his sensitiveness is quickened because they are characters in his novel. It does not at all follow that the same artist would be moved to tears over the report of parallel catastrophes in real life. As an artist, there is every reason to suppose he would welcome the news with downright pleasure. It would be for him "good material." He would see a story in it, a good scene, a great character. Thus the artist. What he would do, how he would feel as a man is quite a different matter.

To conclude, let us consider one objection urged against the novel with a purpose by the plain people who read. For certain reasons, difficult to explain, the purpose novel always ends unhappily. It is usually a record of suffering, a relation of tragedy. And the plain people say, "Ah, we see so much suffering in the world, why put it into novels? We do not want it in novels."

One confesses to very little patience with this sort. "We see so much suffering in the world already!" Do they? Is this really true? The people who buy novels are the well-to-do people. They belong to a class whose whole scheme of life is concerned solely with an aim to avoid the unpleasant. Suffering, the great catastrophes, the social throes, that annihilate whole communities, or that crush even isolated individuals—all these are as far removed from them as earthquakes and tidal-waves. Or, even if it were so, suppose that by some miracle these blind eyes were opened and the sufferings of the poor, the tragedies of the house around the corner, really were laid bare. If there is much pain in life, all the more reason that it should appear in a class of literature which, in its highest form, is a sincere transcription of life.

It is the complaint of the coward, this cry against the novel with a purpose, because it brings the tragedies and griefs of others to notice. Take this element from fiction, take from it the power and opportunity to prove that injustice, crime and inequality do exist, and what is left? Just the amusing novels, the novels that entertain. The juggler in spangles, with his balancing-pole and gilt ball, does this. You may consider the modern novel from this point of view. It may be a flippant paper-covered thing of swords and cloaks, to be carried on a railway journey and to be thrown out the window when read, together with the sucked oranges and peanut shells. Or it may be a great force, that works together with the pulpit and the universities for the good of the people, fearlessly proving that power is abused, that the strong grind the faces of the weak, that an evil tree is still growing in the midst of the garden, that undoing follows hard upon unrighteousness, that the course of Empire is not yet finished, and that the races of men have yet to work out their destiny in those great and terrible movements that crush and grind and rend asunder the pillars of the houses of the nations.

Fiction may keep pace with the Great March, but it will not be by dint of amusing the people. The muse is a teacher, not a trickster. Her rightful place is with the leaders, but in the last analysis that place is to be attained and maintained not by cap-and-bells, but because of a serious and sincere interest, such as inspires the great teachers, the great divines, the great philosophers, a well-defined, well-seen, courageously sought-for purpose.

STORY-TELLERS VS. NOVELISTS

STORY-TELLERS VS. NOVELISTS

IT is a thing accepted and indisputable that a story-teller is a novelist, but it has often occurred to one that the reverse is not always true and that the novelist is not of necessity a story-teller. The distinction is perhaps a delicate one, but for all that it seems to be decisive, and it is quite possible that with the distinction in mind a different judgment might be passed upon a very large part of present-day fiction. It would even be entertaining to apply the classification to the products of the standard authors.

The story-telling instinct seems to be a gift, whereas—we trend to the heretical—the art of composing novels—using the word in apposition to stories, long or short—may be an acquirement. The one is an endowment, the other an accomplishment. Accordingly throughout the following paragraphs the expression, novelists of composition, for the time being will be used technically, and will be applied to those fiction-writers who have not the story-telling faculty.

It would not be fair to attempt a proof that

the one is better or worse than the other. The difference is surely of kind and not of degree. One will only seek to establish the fact that certain eminent and brilliant novel-writers are quite bereft of a sense of fiction, that some of them have succeeded in spite of this deficiency, and that other novel-writers possessing this sense of fiction have succeeded *because* of it, and in spite of many drawbacks such as lack of training and of education.

It is a proposition which one believes to be capable of demonstration that every child contains in himself the elements of every known profession, every occupation, every art, every industry. In the five-year-old you may see glimpses of the soldier, trader, farmer, painter, musician, builder, and so on to the end of the roster. Later, circumstances produce the atrophy of all of these instincts but one, and from that one specialized comes the career. Thus every healthy-minded child—no matter if he develops in later years to be financier or boot-maker—is a story-teller. As soon as he begins to talk he tells stories. Witness the holocausts and carnage of the leaden platoons of the nursery table, the cataclysms of the Grand Trans-Continental Playroom and Front-Hall Railroad system. This, though, is not real story-telling. The toys practically tell the story for him and are no stimulant to the imagination. However, the child goes beyond the toys. He dramatizes every object of his surroundings. The books of the library shelves are files of soldiers, the rugs are isles in the seaway of the floor, the easy chair is a comfortable old gentleman holding out his arms, the sofa a private brig or a Baldwin locomotive, and the child creates of his surroundings an entire and complex work of fiction of which he is at one and the same time hero, author and public.

Within the heart of every mature human being, not a writer of fiction, there is the withered remains of a little story-teller who died very young. And the love of good fiction and the appreciation of a fine novel in the man of the world of riper years is—I like to think—a sort of memorial tribute which he pays to his little dead playmate of so very long ago, who died very quietly with his little broken tin locomotive in his hands on the cruel day when he woke to the realization that it had outlived its usefulness and its charm.

Even in the heart of some accepted and successful fiction-writer you shall find this little dead story-teller. These are the novelists of composition, whose sense of fiction, under stress of circumstances, has become so blunted that when they come at last to full maturity and to the power of using the faculty they can no longer command it. These are novelists rather of intellect than of spontaneous improvisation; and all the force of their spendid minds, every faculty other than the lost fiction-faculty, must be brought into play to compensate for the lack. Some more than compensate for it, so prodigal in resource, so persistent in effort, so powerful in energy and in fertility of invention, that—as it were by main strength—they triumph over the other writer, the natural story-teller, from whose pen the book flows with almost no effort at all.

Of this sort—the novelists of intellect, in whom the born story-teller is extinct, the novelists of composition in a word—the great example, it would seem, is George Eliot. It was by taking thought that the author of "Romola" added to her stature. The result is superb, but achieved at what infinite pains, with what colossal labour—of head rather than of the heart! She did not *feel*, she *knew*, and to attain that knowledge what effort had to be expended! Even all her art cannot exclude from her pages evidences of the labour, of the superhuman toil. And it was labour and toil for what? To get back, through years of sophistication, of solemn education, of worldly wisdom, back again to the point of view of the little lost child of the doll-house days.

But sometimes the little story-teller does not die, but lives on and grows with the man, increasing in favour with God, till at [last he dominates the man himself, and the playroom of the old days simply widens its walls till it includes the street outside, and the street beyond and other streets, the whole city, the whole world, and the story-teller discovers a set of new toys to play with, and new objects of a measureless environment to dramatize about, and in exactly, *exactly* the same spirit in which he trundled his tin train through the halls and shouted boarding orders from the sofa he moves now through the world's play-room "making up stories"; only now his heroes and his public are outside himself and he alone may play the author.

For him there is but little effort required. He has a *sense of fiction*. Every instant of his day he is dramatizing. The cable-car has for him a distinct personality. Every window in the residence quarters is an eye to the soul of the house behind. The very lamp-post on the corner, burning on through the night and through the storm, is a soldier, dutiful, vigilant in stress. A ship is Adventure; an engine a living brute; and the easy chair of his library is still the same comfortable and kindly old gentleman holding out his arms.

The men and women of his world are not apt to be—to him—so important in themselves as in relation to the whirl of things in which he chooses to involve them. They cause events, or else events happen to them, and by an unreasoned instinct the story-teller preserves the consistencies (just as the child would not have run the lines of the hall railway across the seaway of the floor between the rugs). Much thought is not necessary to him. Production is facile, a constant pleasure. The story runs from his pen almost of itself; it takes this shape or that, he knows not why; his people do this or that and by some blessed system of guesswork they are somehow always plausible and true to life. His work is haphazard, yet in the end and in the main tremendously probable. Devil-may-care, slipshod, melodramatic, but invincibly persuasive, he uses his heart, his senses, his emotions, every faculty but that of the intellect. He does not *know;* he *feels*.

Dumas was this, and "The Three Musketeers," different from "Romola" in kind but not in degree, is just as superb as Eliot at her best. Only the Frenchman had a sense of fiction which the Englishwoman had not. Her novels are character studies, are portraits, are portrayals of emotions or pictures of certain times and certain events, are everything you choose, but they are not stories, and no stretch of the imagination, no liberalness of criticism can make them such. She succeeded by dint of effort where the Frenchman—merely wrote.

George Eliot compensated for the defect artificially and succeeded eminently and conclusively, but there are not found wanting cases—in modern literature—where "novelists of composition" have *not* compensated beyond a very justifiable doubt, and where, had they but rejoiced in a very small modicum of this dowry of the gods, their work would have been—to one's notion—infinitely improved.

As, for instance, Tolstoi; incontestably great though he be, all his unquestioned power has never yet won for him that same vivid sense of fiction enjoyed by so (comparatively) unimportant a writer as the author of "Sherlock Holmes." And of the two, judged strictly upon their merits as *story-tellers*, one claims for Mr. Doyle the securer if not the higher place, despite the magnificent genius of the novelist.

In the austere Russian—gloomy, sad, acquainted with grief—the child died irrevocably long, long ago; and no power however vast, no wisdom however profound, no effort however earnest, can turn one wheel on the little locomotive of battered tin or send it one inch along the old right-of-way between the nursery and the front room.   One cannot but feel that the great author of "Anna Karenina" realizes as much as his readers the limitations that the loss of this untainted childishness imposes. The power was all his, the wonderful intellectual grip, but not the fiction spirit—the child's knack and love of "making up stories."   Given *that*, plus the force already his own, and what a book would have been there! The perfect novel! No doubt, clearer than all others, the great Russian sees the partial failure of his work, and no doubt keener and deeper than all others sees that, unless the child-vision and the child-pleasure be present to guide and to stimulate, the entrances of the kingdom must stay forever shut to those who would enter, storm they the gates never so mightily and beat they never so clamorously at the doors.

Whatever the end of fiction may be, whatever the reward and recompense bestowed, whatever object is gained by good work, the end will not be gained, nor the reward won, nor the object attained by force alone—by strength of will or of mind.   Without the auxiliary of the little playmate of the old days the great doors that stand at the end of the road will stay forever shut. Look once, however, with the child's eyes, or for once touch the mighty valves with the child's hand, and Heaven itself lies open with all its manifold wonders.

So that in the end, after all trial has been made and every expedient tested, the simplest way is the best and the humblest means the surest. A little child stands in the midst of the wise men and the learned, and their wisdom and their learning are set aside and they are taught that unless they become as one of these they shall in nowise enter into the Kingdom of Heaven.

THE NEED OF A LITERARY
CONSCIENCE

THE NEED OF A LITERARY CONSCIENCE

PILATE saith unto them: what is truth?"
and it is of record that he received no
answer—and for very obvious reasons. For
is it not a fact, that he who asks that question
must himself find the answer, and that not
even one sent from Heaven can be of hope or
help to him if he is not willing to go down into
his own heart and into his own life to find it?

To sermonize, to elaborate a disquisition on
nice distinctions of metaphysics is not appropriate here. But it is—so one believes—
appropriate to consider a certain very large
class of present day novelists of the United
States who seldom are stirred by that spirit
of inquiry that for a moment disturbed the
Roman, who do *not* ask what is truth, who do
not in fact care to be truthful at all, and who
—and this is the serious side of the business—
are bringing the name of American literature
perilously near to disrepute.

One does not quarrel for one instant with
the fact that certain books of the writers in
question have attaincd phenomenally large
circulations. This is as it should be. There

49

are very many people in the United States, and compared with such a figure as seventy million, a mere hundred thousand of books sold is no great matter.

But here—so it seems—is the point. He who can address a hundred thousand people is, no matter what his message may be, in an important position. It is a large audience, one hundred thousand, larger than any roofed building now standing could contain. Less than one one-hundredth part of that number nominated Lincoln. Less than half of it won Waterloo.

And it must be remembered that for every one person who buys a book there are three who will read it and half a dozen who will read what some one else has written about it, so that the sphere of influence widens indefinitely, and the audience that the writer addresses approaches the half-million mark.

Well and good; but if the audience is so vast, if the influence is so far-reaching, if the example set is so contagious, it becomes incumbent to ask, it becomes imperative to demand that the half-million shall be told the truth and not a lie.

And this thing called truth—"what is it?" says Pilate, and the average man conceives at once of an abstraction, a vague idea, a term borrowed from the metaphysicians, certainly nothing that has to do with practical, tangible, concrete work-a-day life.

Error! If truth is not an actual workaday thing, as concrete as the lamp-post on the corner, as practical as a cable-car, as real and homely and workaday and commonplace as a bootjack, then indeed are we of all men most miserable and our preaching vain.

And truth in fiction is just as real and just as important as truth anywhere else—as in Wall Street, for instance. A man who does not tell the truth there, and who puts the untruth upon paper over his signature, will be very promptly jailed. In the case of the Wall Street man the sum of money in question may be trivial—$100, $50. But the untruthful novelist who starts in motion something like half a million dollars invokes not fear nor yet reproach. If truth in the matter of the producing of novels is not an elusive, intangible abstraction, what, then, is it? Let us get at the hard nub of the business, something we can hold in the hand. It is the thing that is one's own, the discovery of a subject suitable for fictitious narration that has never yet been treated, and the conscientious study of that subject and the fair presentation of results. Not a difficult matter, it would appear, not an abstraction, not a philosophical kink. Newspaper reporters, who are not metaphysicians, unnamed, unrewarded, despised, even, and hooted and hounded, are doing this every day. They do it on a meager salary, and they call the affair a "scoop." Is the standard of the novelist—he who is entrusted with the good name of his nation's literature—lower than that of a reporter?

"Ah, but it is so hard to be original," "ah, but it is so hard to discover anything new." Great Heavens! when a new life comes into the world for every tick of the watch in your pocket—a new life with all its complications, and with all the thousand and one other complications it sets in motion!

Hard to be original! when of all of those billion lives your own is as distinct, as individual, as "original," as though you were born out of season in the Paleozoic age and yours the first human face the sun ever shone upon.

Go out into the street and stand where the ways cross and hear the machinery of life work clashing in its grooves. Can the utmost resort of your ingenuity evolve a better story than any one of the millions that jog your elbow? Shut yourself in your closet and turn your eyes inward upon yourself—deep *into* yourself, down, down into the heart of you;

and the tread of the feet upon the pavement is the systole and diastole of your own being— different only in degree. It is life; and it is that which you must have to make your book, your novel—life, not other people's novels.

Or look from your window. A whole Literature goes marching by, clamouring for a leader and a master hand to guide it. You have but to step from your doorway. And instead of this, instead of entering into the leadership that is yours by right divine, instead of this, you must toilfully, painfully endeavour to crawl into the armour of the chief of some other cause, the harness of the leader of some other progress.

But you will not fit into that panoply. You may never brace that buckler upon your arm, for by your very act you stand revealed as a littler man than he who should be chief— a littler man and a weaker; and the casque will fall so far over your face that it will only blind you, and the sword will trip you, and the lance, too ponderous, will falter in your grip, and all that life which surges and thunders behind you will in time know you to be the false leader, and as you stumble will trample you in its onrush, and leave you dead and forgotten upon the road.

And just as a misconception of the truth

makes of this the simplest and homeliest of things, a vagary, an abstraction and a bugbear, so it is possible that a misconception of the Leader creates the picture of a great and dreadful figure wrapped in majesty, solemn and profound. So that perhaps for very lack of self-confidence, for very diffidence, one shrinks from lifting the sword of him and from enduing one's forehead with the casque that seems so ponderous.

In other causes no doubt the leader must be chosen from the wise and great. In science and finance one looks to him to be a strong man, a swift and a sure man. But the literature that to-day shouts all in vain for its chief needs no such a one as this. Here the battle is not to the strong nor yet the race to the swift. Here the leader is no vast, stern being, profound, solemn, knowing all things, but, on the contrary, is as humble as the lowliest that follow after him. So that it need not be hard to step into that place of eminence. Not by arrogance, nor by assumption, nor by the achievement of the world's wisdom, shall you be made worthy of the place of high command. But it will come to you, if it comes at all, because you shall have kept yourself young and humble and pure in heart, and so unspoiled and unwearied and unjaded that you shall find a joy in the mere rising of the sun, a wholesome, sane delight in the sound of the wind at night, a pleasure in the sight of the hills at evening, shall see God in a little child and a whole religion in a brooding bird.

A NEGLECTED EPIC

A NEGLECTED EPIC

SUDDENLY we have found that there is no longer any Frontier. The westward-moving course of empire has at last crossed the Pacific Ocean. Civilization has circled the globe and has come back to its starting point, the vague and mysterious East.

The thing has not been accomplished peacefully. From the very first it has been an affair of wars—of invasions. Invasions of the East by the West, and of raids North and South— raids accomplished by flying columns that dashed out from both sides of the main army. Sometimes even the invaders have fought among themselves, as for instance the Trojan War, or the civil wars of Italy, England and America; sometimes they have turned back on their tracks and, upon one pretext or another, reconquered the races behind them, as for instance Alexander's wars to the eastward, the Crusades, and Napoleon's Egyptian campaigns.

Retarded by all these obstacles, the march has been painfully slow. To move from Egypt to Greece took centuries of time. More

59

centuries were consumed in the campaign that brought empire from Greece to Rome, and still more centuries passed before it crossed the Alps and invaded northern and western Europe.

But observe. Once across the Mississippi, the West—our Far West—was conquered in about forty years. In all the vast campaign from east to west here is the most signal victory, the swiftest, the completest, the most brilliant achievement—the wilderness subdued at a single stroke.

Now all these various fightings to the westward, these mysterious race-movements, migrations, wars and wanderings have produced their literature, distinctive, peculiar, excellent. And this literature we call epic. The Trojan War gave us the "Iliad," the "Odyssey" and the "Æneid"; the campaign of the Greeks in Asia Minor produced the "Anabasis"; a whole cycle of literature grew from the conquest of Europe after the fall of Rome—"The Song of Roland," "The Nibelungenlied," "The Romance of the Rose," "Beowulf," "Magnusson," "The Scotch Border Ballads," "The Poem of the Cid," "The Hemskringla," "Orlando Furioso," "Jerusalem Delivered," and the like.

On this side of the Atlantic, in his clumsy,

artificial way, but yet recognized as a producer of literature, Cooper has tried to chronicle the conquest of the eastern part of our country. Absurd he may be in his ideas of life and character, the art in him veneered over with charlatanism; yet the man was solemn enough and took his work seriously, and his work is literature.

Also a cycle of romance has grown up around the Civil War. The theme has had its poets to whom the public have been glad to listen. The subject is vast, noble; is, in a word, epic, just as the Trojan War and the Retreat of the Ten Thousand were epic.

But when at last one comes to look for the literature that sprang from and has grown up around the last great epic event in the history of civilization, the event which in spite of stupendous difficulties was consummated more swiftly, more completely, more satisfactorily than any like event since the westward migration began—I mean the conquering of the West, the subduing of the wilderness beyond the Mississippi—What has this produced in the way of literature? The dime novel! The dime novel and nothing else. The dime novel and nothing better.

The Trojan War left to posterity the character of Hector; the wars with the Saracens gave us Roland; the folklore of Iceland produced Grettir; the Scotch border poetry brought forth the Douglas; the Spanish epic the Cid. But the American epic, just as heroic, just as elemental, just as important and as picturesque, will fade into history leaving behind no finer type, no nobler hero than Buffalo Bill.

The young Greeks sat on marble terraces overlooking the Ægean Sea and listened to the thunderous roll of Homer's hexameter. In the feudal castles the minstrel sang to the young boys, of Roland. The farm folk of Iceland to this very day treasure up and read to their little ones hand-written copies of the Gretla Saga chronicling the deeds and death of Grettir the Strong. But the youth of the United States learn of their epic by paying a dollar to see the "Wild West Show."

The plain truth of the matter is that we have neglected our epic—the black shame of it be on us—and no contemporaneous poet or chronicler thought it worth his while to sing the song or tell the tale of the West because literature in the day when the West was being won was a cult indulged in by certain well-bred gentlemen in New England who looked eastward to the Old World, to the legends of England and Norway and Germany and Italy for their inspiration, and left the great, strong, honest, fearless, resolute deeds of their own countrymen to be defamed and defaced by the nameless hacks of the "yellow back" libraries.

One man—who wrote "How Santa Claus Came to Simpson's Bar"—one poet, one chronicler did, in fact, arise for the moment, who understood that wild, brave life and who for a time gave promise of bearing record of things seen.

One of the requirements of an epic—a true epic—is that its action must devolve upon some great national event. There was no lack of such in those fierce years after '49. Just that long and terrible journey from the Mississippi to the ocean is an epic in itself. Yet no serious attempt has ever been made by an American author to render into prose or verse this event in our history as "national" in scope, in origin and in results as the Revolution itself. The prairie schooner is as large a figure in the legends as the black ship that bore Ulysses homeward from Troy. The sea meant as much to the Argonauts of the fifties as it did to the ten thousand.

And the Alamo! There is a trumpet-call in the word; and only the look of it on the printed page is a flash of fire. But the very histories slight the deed, and to many an

American, born under the same flag that the Mexican rifles shot to ribbons on that splendid day, the word is meaningless.   Yet Thermopylæ was less glorious, and in comparison with that siege the investment of Troy was mere wanton riot.   At the very least the Texans in that battered adobe church fought for the honour of their flag and the greater glory of their country, not for loot or the possession of the person of an adultress.   Young men are taught to consider the " Iliad," with its butcheries, its glorification of inordinate selfishness and vanity, as a classic.   Achilles, murderer, egoist, ruffian and liar, is a hero.   But the name of Bowie, the name of the man who gave his life to his flag at the Alamo, is perpetuated only in the designation of a knife.   Crockett is the hero only of a "funny story" about a sagacious coon; while Travis, the boy commander who did what Gordon with an empire back of him failed to do, is quietly and definitely ignored.

Because we have done nothing to get at the truth about the West; because our best writers have turned to the old-country folklore and legends for their inspiration; because "melancholy harlequins" strut in fringed leggings upon the street-corners, one hand held out for pennies, we have come to believe that our West, our epic, was an affair of Indians, road-agents and desperadoes, and have taken no account of the brave men who stood for law and justice and liberty, and for those great ideas died by the hundreds, unknown and unsung—died that the West might be subdued, that the last stage of the march should be accomplished, that the Anglo-Saxon should fulfil his destiny and complete the cycle of the world.

The great figure of our neglected epic, the Hector of our ignored Iliad, is not, as the dime novels would have us believe, a lawbreaker, but a lawmaker; a fighter, it is true, as is always the case with epic figures, but a fighter for peace, a calm, grave, strong man who hated the lawbreaker as the hound hates the wolf.

He did not lounge in barrooms; he did not cheat at cards; he did not drink himself to maudlin fury; he did not "shoot at the drop of the hat." But he loved his horse, he loved his friend, he was kind to little children; he was always ready to side with the weak against the strong, with the poor against the rich. For hypocrisy and pretense, for shams and subterfuges he had no mercy, no tolerance. He was too brave to lie and too strong to steal. The odds in that lawless day were ever against him; his enemies were many and his friends were few; but his face was always set bravely against evil, and fear was not in him even at the end.   For such a man as this could die no quiet death in a land where law went no further than the statute books and life lay in the crook of my neighbour's forefinger.

He died in defense of an ideal, an epic hero, a legendary figure, formidable, sad.   He died facing down injustice, dishonesty and crime; died "in his boots"; and the same world that has glorified Achilles and forgotten Travis finds none too poor to do him reverence.   No literature has sprung up around him—this great character native to America.   He is of all the world-types the one distinctive to us— peculiar, particular and unique.   He is dead and even his work is misinterpreted and misunderstood.   His very memory will soon be gone, and the American epic, which, on the shelves of posterity, should have stood shoulder to shoulder with the "Hemskringla" and the "Tales of the Nibelungen" and the "Song of Roland," will never be written.

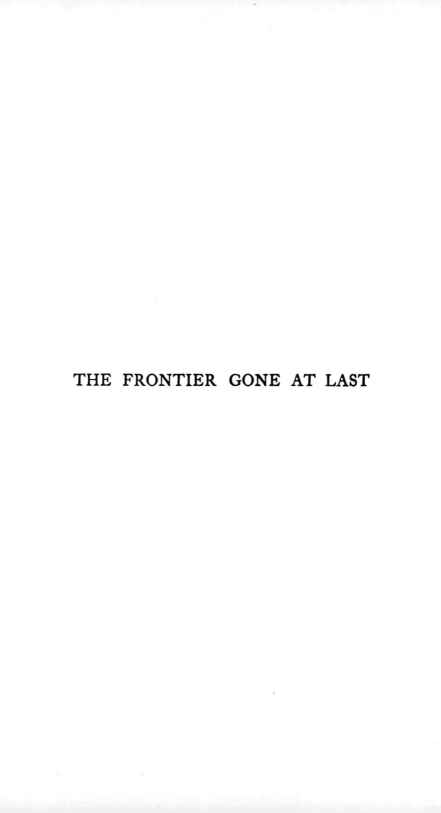

THE FRONTIER GONE AT LAST

THE FRONTIER GONE AT LAST

UNTIL the day when the first United States marine landed in China we had always imagined that out yonder somewhere in the West was the borderland where civilization disintegrated and merged into the untamed. Our skirmish-line was there, our posts that scouted and scrimmaged with the wilderness, a thousand miles in advance of the steady march of civilization.

And the Frontier has become so much an integral part of our conception of things that it will be long before we shall all understand that it is gone. We liked the Frontier; it was romance, the place of the poetry of the Great March, the firing-line where there was action and fighting, and where men held each other's lives in the crook of the forefinger. Those who had gone out came back with tremendous tales, and those that stayed behind made up other and even more tremendous tales.

When we—we Anglo-Saxons—busked ourselves for the first stage of the march, we began from that little historic reach of ground

in the midst of the Friesland swamps, and we
set our faces Westward, feeling no doubt the
push of the Slav behind us.   Then the Frontier
was Britain and the sober peacefulness of land
where are the ordered, cultivated English farm-
yards of to-day was the Wild West of the
Frisians of that century; and for the little children of the Frisian peat cottages Hengist was
the Apache Kid and Horsa Deadwood Dick—
freebooters, law-defiers, slayers-of-men, epic
heroes, blood brothers, if you please, of Boone
and Bowie.

Then for centuries we halted and the van
closed up with the firing-line, and we filled all
England and all Europe with our clamour
because for awhile we seemed to have gone
as far Westward as it was possible; and the
checked energy of the race reacted upon itself,
rebounded as it were, and back we went to the
Eastward again—crusading, girding at the
Mahommedan, conquering his cities, breaking
into his fortresses with mangonel, siege-engine
and catapult—just as the boy shut indoors
finds his scope circumscribed and fills the
whole place with the racket of his activity.

But always, if you will recall it, we had a
curious feeling that we had not reached the
ultimate West even yet, and there was still a
Frontier.   Always that strange sixth sense

turned our heads toward the sunset; and all through the Middle Ages we were peeking and prying into the Western horizon, trying to reach it, to run it down, and the queer tales about Vineland and that storm-driven Viking's ship would not down.

And then at last a naked savage on the shores of a little island in what is now our West Indies, looking Eastward one morning, saw the caravels, and on that day the Frontier was rediscovered, and promptly a hundred thousand of the more hardy rushed to the skirmish-line and went at the wilderness as only the Anglo-Saxon can.

And then the skirmish-line decided that it would declare itself independent of the main army behind and form an advance column of its own, a separate army corps; and no sooner was this done than again the scouts went forward, went Westward, pushing the Frontier ahead of them, scrimmaging with the wilderness, blazing the way. At last they forced the Frontier over the Sierra Nevadas down to the edge of the Pacific. And here it would have been supposed that the Great March would have halted again as it did before the Atlantic, that here at last the Frontier ended.

But on the first of May, 1898, a gun was fired in the Bay of Manila, still farther Westward, and in response the skirmish-line crossed the Pacific, still pushing the Frontier before it. Then came a cry for help from Legation Street in Peking, and as the first boat bearing its contingent of American marines took ground on the Asian shore, the Frontier—at last after so many centuries, after so many marches, after so much fighting, so much spilled blood, so much spent treasure, dwindled down and vanished; for the Anglo-Saxon in his course of empire had circled the globe and brought the new civilization to the old civilization, and reached the starting point of history, the place from which the migrations began. So soon as the marines landed there was no longer any West, and the equation of the horizon, the problem of the centuries for the Anglo-Saxon was solved.

So, lament it though we may, the Frontier is gone, an idiosyncrasy that has been with us for thousands of years, the one peculiar picturesqueness of our life is no more. We may keep alive for many years the idea of a Wild West, but the hired cowboys and paid rough riders of Mr. William Cody are more like "the real thing" than can be found to-day in Arizona, New Mexico or Idaho. Only the imitation cowboys, the college-bred fellows who "go out on a ranch," carry the revolver or wear the concho. The Frontier has become conscious of itself, acts the part for the Eastern visitor; and this self-consciousness is a sign, surer than all others, of the decadence of a type, the passing of an epoch. The Apache Kid and Deadwood Dick have gone to join Hengist and Horsa and the heroes of the Magnusson Saga.

But observe. What happened in the Middle Ages when for awhile we could find no Western Frontier? The race impulse was irresistible. March we must, conquer we must, and checked in the Westward course of empire, we turned Eastward and expended the resistless energy that by blood was ours in conquering the Old World behind us.

To-day we are the same race, with the same impulse, the same power and, because there is no longer a Frontier to absorb our overplus of energy, because there is no longer a wilderness to conquer and because we still must march, still must conquer, we remember the old days when our ancestors before us found the outlet for their activity checked and, rebounding, turned their faces Eastward, and went down to invade the Old World. So we. No sooner have we found that our path to the Westward has ended than, reacting Eastward, we are at the Old World again, marching against it, invading it, devoting our overplus of energy to its subjugation.

But though we are the same race, with the same impulses, the same blood-instincts as the old Frisian marsh people, we are now come into a changed time and the great word of our century is no longer War, but Trade.

Or, if you choose, it is only a different word for the same race-characteristic. The desire for conquest—say what you will—was as big in the breast of the most fervid of the Crusaders as it is this very day in the most peacefully disposed of American manufacturers. Had the Lion-Hearted Richard lived to-day he would have become a "leading representative of the Amalgamated Steel Companies," and doubt not for one moment that he would have underbid his Manchester rivals in the matter of bridge-girders. Had Mr. Andrew Carnegie been alive at the time of the preachings of Peter the Hermit he would have raised a company of *gens d'armes* sooner than all of his brothers-in-arms, would have equipped his men better and more effectively, would have been first on the ground before Jerusalem, would have built the most ingenious siege-engine and have hurled the first cask of Greek-fire over the walls.

Competition and conquest are words easily interchangeable, and the whole spirit of our present commercial crusade to the Eastward betrays itself in the fact that we cannot speak of it but in terms borrowed from the glossary of the warrior. It is a commercial "invasion," a trade "war," a "threatened attack" on the part of America; business is "captured," opportunities are "seized," certain industries are "killed," certain former monopolies are "wrested away." Seven hundred years ago a certain Count Baldwin, a great leader in the attack of the Anglo-Saxon Crusaders upon the Old World, built himself a siege-engine which would help him enter the beleaguered city of Jerusalem. Jerusalem is beleaguered again to-day, and the hosts of the Anglo-Saxon commercial crusaders are knocking at the gates. And now a company named for another Baldwin—and, for all we know, a descendant of the Count—leaders of the invaders of the Old World, advance upon the city, and, to help in the assault, build an engine—only now the engine is no longer called a *mangonel*, but a locomotive.

The difference is hardly of kind and scarcely of degree. It is a mere matter of names, and the ghost of Saladin watching the present engagement might easily fancy the old days back again.

So perhaps we have not lost the Frontier,

after all. A new phrase, reversing that of
Berkeley's, is appropriate to the effect that
"Eastward the course of commerce takes its
way," and we must look for the lost battle-
line not toward the sunset, but toward the
East. And so rapid has been the retrograde
movement that we must go far to find it, that
scattered firing-line, where the little skirmishes
are heralding the approach of the Great March.
We must already go farther afield than England.
The main body, even to the reserves, are
intrenched there long since, and even continental Europe is to the rear of the skirmishers.

Along about Suez we begin to catch up with
them where they are deepening the great canal,
and we can assure ourselves that we are fairly
abreast of the most distant line of scouts only
when we come to Khiva, to Samarcand, to
Bokhara and the Trans-Baikal country.

Just now one hears much of the "American
commercial invasion of England." But adjust
the field-glasses and look beyond Britain and
seach for the blaze that the scouts have left
on the telegraph poles and mile-posts of
Hungary, Turkey, Turkey in Asia, Persia,
Baluchistan, India and Siam. You'll find the
blaze distinct and the road, though rough hewn,
is easy to follow. Prophecy and presumption
be far from us, but it would be against all

precedent that the Grand March should rest forever upon its arms and its laurels along the Thames, the Mersey and the Clyde, while its pioneers and frontiersmen are making roads for it to the Eastward.

Is it too huge a conception, too inordinate an idea to say that the American conquest of England is but an incident of the Greater Invasion, an affair of outposts preparatory to the real maneuver that shall embrace Europe, Asia, the whole of the Old World? Why not? And the blaze is ahead of us, and every now and then from far off there in the countries that are under the rising sun we catch the faint sounds of the skirmishing of our outposts. One of two things invariably happens under such circumstances as these: either the outposts fall back upon the main body or the main body moves up to the support of its outposts. One does not think that the outposts will fall back.

And so goes the great movement, Westward, then Eastward, forward and then back. The motion of the natural forces, the elemental energies, somehow appear to be thus alternative—action first, then reaction. The tides ebb and flow again, the seasons have their slow vibrations, touching extremes at periodic intervals. Not impossibly, in the larger view, is the analogy applicable to the movements of the races. First Westward with the great migrations, now Eastward with the course of commerce, moving in a colossal arc measured only by the hemispheres, as though upon the equator a giant dial hand oscillated, in gradual divisions through the centuries, now marking off the Westward progress, now traveling proportionately to the reaction toward the East.

Races must follow their destiny blindly, but is it not possible that we can find in this great destiny of ours something a little better than mere battle and conquest, something a little more generous than mere trading and underbidding? Inevitably with constant change of environment comes the larger view, the more tolerant spirit, and every race movement, from the first step beyond the Friesland swamp to the adjustment of the first American theodolite on the Himalayan watershed, is an unconscious lesson in patriotism. Just now we cannot get beyond the self-laudatory mood, but is it not possible to hope that, as the progress develops, a new patriotism, one that shall include all peoples, may prevail? The past would indicate that this is a goal toward which we trend.

In the end let us take the larger view, ignoring the Frieslanders, the Anglo-Saxons, the

Americans. Let us look at the peoples as
people and observe how inevitably as they
answer the great Westward impulse the true
patriotism develops. If we can see that it is
so with all of them we can assume that it must
be so with us, and may know that mere victory
in battle as we march Westward, or mere
supremacy in trade as we react to the East,
is not after all the great achievement of the
races, but patriotism. Not our present selfish
day conception of the word, but a new patriotism, whose meaning is now the secret of the
coming centuries.

Consider then the beginnings of patriotism.
At the very first, the seed of the future nation
was the regard of family; the ties of common
birth held men together, and the first feeling
of patriotism was the love of family. But the
family grows, develops by lateral branches,
expands and becomes the clan. Patriotism is
the devotion to the clan, and the clansmen
will fight and die for its supremacy.

Then comes the time when the clans, tired
of the roving life of herders, halt a moment
and settle down in a chosen spot; the tent,
becoming permanent, evolves the dwelling-
house, and the encampment of the clan becomes
at last a city. Patriotism now is civic pride;
the clan absorbed into a multitude of clans is

forgotten; men speak of themselves as Athenians, not as Greeks, as Romans, not as Italians. It is the age of cities.

The city extends its adjoining grazing fields; they include outlying towns, other cities, and finally the State comes into being. Patriotism no longer confines itself to the walls of the city, but is enlarged to encompass the entire province. Men are Hanoverians or Wurtemburgers, not Germans; Scots or Welsh, not English; are even Carolinians or Alabamans rather than Americans.

But the States are federated, pronounced boundaries fade, State makes common cause with State, and at last the nation is born. Patriotism at once is a national affair, a far larger, broader, truer sentiment than that first huddling about the hearthstone of the family. The word "brother" may be applied to men unseen and unknown, and a countryman is one of many millions.

We have reached this stage at the present, but if all signs are true, if all precedent may be followed, if all augury may be relied on and the tree grow as we see the twig is bent, the progress will not stop here.

By war to the Westward the family fought its way upward to the dignity of the nation; by reaction Eastward the nation may in patriotic effect merge with other nations, and others and still others, peacefully, the bitterness of trade competition may be lost, the business of the nations seen as a friendly *quid pro quo*, give and take arrangement, guided by a generous reciprocity. Every century the boundaries are widening, patriotism widens with the expansion, and our countrymen are those of different race, even different nations.

Will it not go on, this epic of civilization, this destiny of the races, until at last and at the ultimate end of all we who now arrogantly boast ourselves as Americans, supreme in conquest, whether of battle-ship or of bridge-building, may realize that the true patriotism is the brotherhood of man and know that the whole world is our nation and simple humanity our countrymen?

THE GREAT AMERICAN
NOVELIST

THE GREAT AMERICAN NOVELIST

OF all the overworked phrases of over-worked book reviewers, the phrase, the "Great American Novelist," is beyond doubt worn the thinnest from much handling—or mishandling. Continually the little literary middlemen who come between the producers and the consumers of fiction are mouthing the words with a great flourish of adjectives, scare-heading them in Sunday supplements or pla-carding them on posters, crying out, "Lo, he is here !" or "lo, there !" But the heathen rage and the people imagine a vain thing. The G. A. N. is either as extinct as the Dodo or as far in the future as the practical aeroplane. He certainly is not discoverable at the present.

The moment a new writer of fiction begins to make himself felt he is gibbeted upon this elevation—upon this *false*, insecure elevation, for the underpinning is of the flimsiest, and at any moment is liable to collapse under the victim's feet and leave him hanging in midair by head and hands, a fixture and a mockery.

And who is to settle the title upon the aspi-rant in the last issue ? Who is to determine what constitutes the G. A. N.   Your candidate may suit *you*, but your neighbour may have a very different standard to which he must conform.   It all depends upon what you mean by *Great*, what you mean by *American*.   Shakespeare has been called great, and so has Mr. Stephen Phillips.   Oliver Wendell Holmes was *American*, and so is Bret Harte.   Who is to say?

And many good people who deplore the decay of American letters are accustomed to refer to the absence of a G. A. N. as though there were a Great English Novelist or a Great French Novelist.   But do these two people exist?   Ask any dozen of your friends to mention the Great English Novelist, and out of the dozen you will get at least a half-dozen different names.   It will be Dickens or Scott or Thackeray or Bronte or Eliot or Stevenson, and the same with the Frenchman.   And it seems to me that if a novelist were great enough to be universally acknowledged to be the Great one of his country, he would cease to belong to any particular geographical area and would become a heritage of the whole world; as for instance Tolstoi; when one thinks of him it is—is it not?—as a novelist first and as a Russian afterward.

But if one wishes to split hairs, one might

admit that while the Great American Novelist is yet to be born, the possibility of *A*—note the indefinite article—*A* Great American Novel is not too remote for discussion. But such a novel will be sectional. The United States is a Union, but not a unit, and the life in one part is very, very different from the life in another. It is as yet impossible to construct a novel which will represent all the various characteristics of the different sections. It is only possible to make a picture of a single locality. What is true of the South is not true of the North. The West is different, and the Pacific Coast is a community by itself.

Many of our very best writers are working on this theory. Bret Harte made a study of the West as he saw it, and Mr. Howells has done the same for the East. Cable has worked the field of the Far South, and Eggleston has gone deep into the life of the Middle West.

But consider a suggestion. It is an argument on the other side, and to be fair one must present it. It is a good argument, and if based on fact is encouraging in the hope that the *Great* man may yet appear. It has been said that "what is true—vitally and inherently true—for any one man is true for all men." Accordingly, then, what is vitally true of the Westerner is true of the Bostonian—yes, and of the creole.   So that if Mr. Cable, say, should only go *deep enough* into the hearts and lives of his creoles, he would at last strike the universal substratum and find the elemental thing that is common to the creole and to the Puritan alike—yes, and to the Cowboy and Hoosier and Greaser and Buckeye and Jay Hawker, and that, once getting hold of *that*, he could produce the Great American Novel that should be a picture of the entire nation.

Now, that is a very ingenious argument and sounds very plausible.   But it won't do, and for this reason: If an American novelist should go so deep into the lives of the people of any one community that he would find the thing that is common to another class of people a thousand miles away, he would have gone *too* deep to be exclusively American.   He would not only be American, but English as well.   He would have sounded the world-note; he would be a writer not national, but international, and his countrymen would be all humanity, not the citizens of any one nation. He himself would be a heritage of the whole world, a second Tolstoi, which brings us back to the very place from which we started.

And the conclusion of the whole matter? That fiction is very good or very bad—there is no middle ground; that writers of fiction in

their points of view are either limited to a circumscribed area or see humanity as a tremendous conglomerate whole; that it must be
either Mary Wilkins or George Eliot, Edward
Eggleston or William Shakespeare; that the
others do not weigh very much in the balance
of the world's judgment; and that the Great
American Novel is not extinct like the Dodo,
but mythical like the Hippogriff, and that the
thing to be looked for is not the Great American
Novelist, but the Great Novelist who shall also
be an American.

NEW YORK AS A LITERARY CENTRE

NEW YORK AS A LITERARY CENTRE

IT has been given to the present writer to know a great many of what one may call The Unarrived in literary work, and of course to be one himself of that "innumerable caravan," and speaking authoritatively and of certain knowledge, the statement may be made, that of all the ambitions of the Great Unpublished, the one that is strongest, the most abiding, is the ambition to get to New York. For these, New York is the "point de depart," the pedestal, the niche, the indispensable vantage ground; as one of the unpublished used to put it: "It is a place that I can stand on and holler."

This man lived in a second-class town west of the Mississippi, and one never could persuade him that he might holler from his own, his native heath, and yet be heard. He said it would be "the voice of one crying in the wilderness." New York was the place for him. Once land him in New York and all would be gas and gaiters.

There are so many thousands like this young man of mine that a word in this connection seems appropriate; and the object of this present writing is to protest against this blind and unreasoned hegira, and to urge the point that tradition, precedent to the contrary notwithstanding, New York is not a literary centre.

I am perfectly well aware that this statement savours of hearsay, but at the same time I think it can be defended. As for instance:

Time was when Boston claimed the distinction that one now denies to New York. But one asserts that Boston made her claims good. In those days the reactionary movement of populations from the cities toward the country had not set in. A constant residence winter and summer in the country was not dreamed of by those who had the leisure and the money to afford it. As much as possible the New England writers crowded to Boston, or to Cambridge, which is practically the same thing, and took root in the place. There was their local habitation; there they lived, and thence they spread their influence. Remember that at the height of the development of the New England school there were practically no other writers of so great importance the length and breadth of the land. This huddling about a common point made it possible to visit all the homes of nearly all of the most eminent

American literati in a single day. The younger
men, the aspirants, the Unpublished, however,
thrown into such society, could not fail to be
tremendously impressed, and, banded together
as these great ones were, their influence counted
enormously. It was no unusual sight to see
half a dozen of these at the same dinner table.
They all knew each other intimately, these
Bostonians, and their word was *Lex*, and the
neophites came from all corners of the compass
to hear them speak, and Boston did in good
earnest become the Hub, the centre of Literary
thought and work in the United States.

But no such conditions obtain in New York
to-day. During the last ten years two very
important things have happened that bear upon
this question. First has come the impulse
toward a country life—a continued winter and
summer residence in the country. Authors
more than any other class of workers can afford
this since their profession can be carried anywhere. They need no city offices. They
are not forced to be in touch with the actual
business life of Broadway. Secondly, since
the days of the Bostonian supremacy a tremendous wave of literary production has
swept over the United States. Now England
has ceased to be the only place where books are
written. Poems are now indited in Dakota,

novels composed in Wyoming, essays written in Utah, and criticisms flourish in Kansas. A thousand and one Little Centres have sprung up. Literary groups are formed everywhere, in Buffalo, in San Francisco, in Indianapolis and Chicago.

All this detracts from the preponderance of any one city, such as New York, as Literary dictator. You shall find but a very small and meager minority of the Greater Men of Letters who have their homes in Manhattan. Most of them preferred to live in the places whereof they treat in their books, in New Orleans, in Indiana, in Kentucky, or Virginia, or California, or Kansas, or Illinois. If they come to New York at all it is only temporarily, to place their newest book or to arrange with publishers for future work.

The result of this is as is claimed. New York is not a literary centre. The publishing houses are there, the magazines, all the distributing machinery, but not the writers. They do not live there. They do not care to come there. They regard the place simply as a distributing point for their wares.

Literary centres produce literary men. Paris, London and Boston all have their long lists of native-born writers—men who were born in these cities and whose work was identified with them. But New York can claim but ridiculously few of the men of larger caliber as her own. James Whitcomb Riley is from Indiana, Joel Chandler Harris is a Southerner. Howells came from Boston, Cable from New Orleans, Hamlin Garland from the West. Bret Harte from California, Mark Twain from the Middle West, Harold Frederic and Henry James found England more congenial than the greatest city of their native land. Even among the younger generation there are but few who can be considered as New Yorkers. Although Richard Harding Davis wrote accurately and delightfully of New York people, he was not born in New York, did not receive his first impetus from New York influences, and does not now live in New York. Nor is his best work upon themes or subjects in any way related to New York.

In view of all these facts it is difficult to see what the Great Unpublished have to gain by a New York residence. Indeed, it is much easier to see how very much they have to lose.

The writing of fiction has many drawbacks, but one of its blessed compensations is the fact that of all the arts it is the most independent. Independent of time, of manner and of place. Wherever there is a table and quiet, there the novel may be written. "Ah, but the publishing houses are in New York." What has that to do with it? Do not for a moment suppose that your novel will be considered more carefully because you submit it in person. It is not as though you were on the lookout for odd jobs which, because of a personal acquaintance with editors and publishers, might be put in your way. The article, the story, the essay, poem or novel is just as good, just as available, just as salable whether it comes from Washington Territory or Washington Square.

Not only this, but one believes that actual residence in New York is hostile and inimical to good work. The place, admittedly, teems with literary clubs, circles, associations, organizations of pseudo-literati, who foregather at specified times to "read papers" and "discuss questions." It is almost impossible for the young writer who comes for a first time to the city to avoid entangling himself with them; and of the influences that tend to stultify ambition, warp original talent and definably and irretrievably stamp out the last spark of productive ability one knows of none more effective than the literary clubs.

You will never find the best men at these gatherings. You will never hear the best work read in this company, you will never evolve any original, personal, definite ideas or ideals under such influence. The discussions of the literary clubs are made up of puerile arguments that have done duty for years in the college text-books. Their work—the papers quoted and stories read aloud—is commonplace and conventional to the deadliest degree, while their "originality"—the ideas that they claim are their very own—is nothing but a distortion and dislocation of preconceived notions, mere bizarre effects of the grotesque and the improbable. "Ah, but the spur of competition." Competition is admirable in trade— it is even desirable in certain arts. It has no place in a literary career. It is not as though two or more writers were working on the same story, each striving to better the others. That would, indeed, be true competition. But in New York, where the young writer—any writer—may see a dozen instances in a week of what he knows is inferior work succeeding where he fails, competition is robbed of all stimulating effect and, if one is not very careful, leaves only the taste of ashes in the mouth and rancour and discontent in the heart.

With other men's novels the novelist has little to do. What this writer is doing, what that one is saying, what books this publishing house is handling, how many copies so-and-so's book is selling—all this fuss and feathers

of "New York as a literary centre" should be
for him so many distractions. It is all very
well to say "let us keep in touch with the
best thought in our line of work." "Let us be
in the movement." The best thought is not
in New York; and even if it were, the best
thought of other men is not so good for you as
your own thought, dug out of your own vitals
by your own unaided efforts, be it never so
inadequate.

You do not have to go to New York for that.
Your own ideas, your own work will flourish
best if left alone untrammeled and uninfluenced.
And believe this to be true, that wherever
there is a table, a sheet of paper and a pot of
ink, there is a Literary Centre if you will. You
will find none better the world over.

THE AMERICAN PUBLIC AND "POPULAR" FICTION

THE AMERICAN PUBLIC AND "POPU-
LAR" FICTION

THE American people judged by Old World
standards—even sometimes according
to native American standards—have always
been considered a practical people, a material
people.

We have been told and have also told ourselves that we are hard-headed, that we rejoiced
in facts and not in fancies, and as an effect of
this characteristic were not given to books.
We were not literary, we assumed, were not
fond of reading. We, who were subjugating
a continent, who were inventing machinery
and building railroads, left it to the older and
more leisurely nations—to France and to
England to read books.

On the face of it this would seem a safe
assumption. As a matter of fact, the American
people are the greatest readers in the world.
That is to say, that, count for count, there
are more books read in the United States in one
year than in any other country of the globe in
the same space of time.

Nowhere do the circulations attain such

magnitude as they do with us.   A little while ago—ten years ago—the charge that we did not read was probably true.   But there must exist some mysterious fundamental connection between this recent sudden expansion of things American—geographic, commercial and other-wise—and the demand for books.   Imperialism, Trade Expansion, the New Prosperity and the Half Million Circulation all came into existence at about the same time.

Merely the fact of great prosperity does not account for the wider reading.   Prosperous periods, good prices, easy credit and a mobile currency have occurred often before without producing the demand for books.   Something more than prosperity has suddenly swept across the continent and evaded the spirit of the times.   Something very like an awakening, something very like a renaissance and the 70,000,000 have all at once awakened to the fact that there are books to be read.   As with all things sudden, there is noticeable with this awakening a lack of discrimination, the 70,000,000 are so eager for books that, *faute de mieux*, anything printed will pass current for literature.   It is a great animal, this American public, and having starved for so long, it is ready, once aroused, to devour anything.   And the great presses of the country are for the most part merely sublimated sausage machines that go dashing along in a mess of paper and printer's ink turning out the meat for the monster.

There are not found wanting many who deplore this and who blackguard the great brute for his appetite. Softly, softly. If the Megatherium has been obliged to swallow wind for sustenance for several hundred years, it would be unkind to abuse him because he eats the first lot of spoiled hay or over-ripe twigs that is thrust under the snout of him. Patience and shuffle the cards. Once his belly filled, and the pachyderm will turn to the new-mown grass and fruit trees in preference to the hay and twigs.

So the studios and the Browning classes need not altogether revile the great American public. Better bad books than no books; better half a loaf of hard bread than *no* frosted wedding-cake. The American people, unlike the English, unlike the French and other Europeans, have not been educated and refined and endoctrinated for 2,000 years, and when you remember what they have done in *one hundred* years, tamed an entire continent, liberated a race, produced a Lincoln, invented the telegraph, spanned the plains—when you remember all this, do not spurn the 70,000,000 because they do not understand Henry James, but be glad that they

even care for "The Duchess" and "Ouida."
The wonder of it is not that they do not read
or appreciate the best, but that they have set
apart any time at all in the struggle of civiliz-
ing the wilderness and forging steel rivets to
so much as pick up any kind or description of
a book.

Consider the other nations, France for
instance—the very sanctum of Art, the home
and birthplace of literature. Compare the
rural districts of France with the rural districts of the United States, and in the comparison allow, if you like, for all the centuries
of quiet uninterrupted growth, the wilderness
tamed, life domesticated, reduced to routine
that modern France enjoys. Do you suppose for
one moment that a bourgeois family of—say—
Tours is on the same level in the matter of
its reading as the household of a contractor's
family in—for example—Martinez, California,
or Cheyenne, Wyoming?

I tell you there is no comparison whatever.
The West may be wild even yet, may be what
Boston would call uncultured, but it *reads*.
There are people in Cheyenne and Martinez
who can express an opinion—and a more
intelligent opinion, mark you—on Maeterlinck
and Bourget, better than the same class of
readers in Belgium and France. And quite

as likely as not the same class of people in the very native countries of the two writers named have never so much as heard of these writers.

This, admittedly, is the exception, but if our exceptional Martinez and Cheyenne people are so far advanced in literary criticism, we may reasonably expect that the rank and file below them are proportionately well on. Maeterlinck and Bourget are closed books to those rank-and-file readers yet. But again I say, this is not the point. The point is, that they are readers at all. Let them—in the name of future American literature—read their Duchesses and Ouidas and Edna Lyalls and Albert Rosses. What are their prototypes in France, Germany and Russia reading? They simply are not reading at all, and as often as not it is not because of the lack of taste, but because of the lack of sheer downright ability, because they do not know how to read.

A very great man once said that "books never have done harm," and under this sign let us conquer. There is hardly a better to be found. Instead, then, of deploring the vast circulation of mediocre novels, let us take the larger view and find in the fact not a weakness, but a veritable strength. The more one reads—it is a curious consolatory fact— the more one is apt to discriminate. The ten-year-old who reads "Old Sleuth" to-day, in a little while will find Scott more to his liking. Just now the 70,000,000 is ten years old.   But it is started right. Patience. Books have never done harm, and in the end let us be certain that the day will come when the real masterpiece, the real literature, will also be selling in its "five hundredth thousand."

CHILD STORIES FOR ADULTS

CHILD STORIES FOR ADULTS

THERE was a time, none too remote at this date of writing, when juvenile and adult fiction were two separate and distinct classifications. Boys read stories for boys and girls stories for girls, and the adults contented themselves with the wise lucubrations of their equals in years. But the last few years have changed all that—have changed everything in American literature, in fact.

Some far-distant day, when the critics and *litterateurs* of the twenty-second and twenty-third centuries shall be writing of our day and age, they will find a name for the sudden and stupendous demand for reading matter that has penetrated to all classes and corners since 1890. A great deal could be said upon this sudden demand in itself, and I think it can be proved to be the first effects of a genuine awakening—a second Renaissance. But the subject would demand an article by itself, and in the meanwhile we may use the term awakening as a self-evident fact and consider not so much the cause as the effects.

One of the effects, as has been already suggested, is the change in classifications. Old forms and formulas are, or are being rapidly broken up, and one school and style merging into others, till now what was once amusement for the children has become entertaining for the elders. And vice versa. The abruptness of the awakening has disjointed and inverted all the old fabric. "Robinson Crusoe," written for adults, is now exclusively a "juvenile," while "Treasure Island," written for boys, has been snapped up by the parents.

Simultaneously with this topsy-turvy business, and I am sure in some way connected with it, comes the craze for stories about very young children for adult reading. A boy's story must now be all about the doings of men, fighters preferably, man-slayers, terrible fellows full of blood and fury, stamping on their quarter-decks or counting doubloons by torch-light on unnamed beaches. Meanwhile the boy's father with a solemn interest is following the fortunes of some terrible infant of the kindergarten, or the vagaries of a ten-year-old of a country town, or the teacup tragedy of "The Very Little Girl," or "The Indiscretion of Pinky Trevethan," or "The Chastening of Skinny McCleave," etc., etc.

It is interesting to try to account for this. It may either be a fad or a phase. It is almost too soon to tell, but in either case the matter is worth considering.

Roughly speaking, the Child's Stories for Adults fall into three classes. First there is "The Strange Child Story." This is a very old favourite, and was pretty well installed long before the more recent developments. In "The Strange Child Story" the bid for the reader's pity and sympathy fairly clamoured from between the lines. Always and persistently The Strange Child was misunderstood. He had "indefinable longings" that were ridiculed, budding talents that were nipped, heartaches — terrible, tear-compelling heartaches—that were ignored; and he lived in an atmosphere of gloom, hostility and loneliness that would have maddened an eremite.

But as his kind declined in popular estimate the country boy, the ten-year-old—who always went in swimmin' and lost his tow—appeared in the magazines. There is no sentiment about him. Never a tear need be shed over the vicarious atonements of Pinky Trevethan or Skinny McCleave.

It is part of the game to pretend that the Pinkys and Skinnys and Peelys and Mickeys are different individuals. Error. They are merely different names of the boy that perennially and persistently remains the same. Do you know who he is? He is the average American business man before he grew up. That accounts for his popularity. The average business man had clean forgotten all about those early phases of primitive growth, and it amuses him immensely to find out that the scribe has been making a study of him and bringing to light the forgotten things that are so tremendously familiar when presented to the consideration. It is not fiction nor yet literature in the straightest sense of the word, this rehabilitation of Skinny McCleave. It has a value vaguely scientific, the same value that a specimen, a fossil insect, has when brought to the attention of the savant. It is the study of an extinct species, a report upon the American boy of thirty years ago.

Then lastly—the latest development—there is the cataclysm of the kindergarten, the checked apron drama, the pigtail passion, the epic of the broken slate-pencil. This needs a delicacy of touch that only a woman can supply, and as a matter of fact it is for the most part women who sign the stories. The interest in these is not so personal and retrospective as in the Skinny McCleave circle, for the kindergarten is too recent to be part of the childhood memories of the present generation of adult magazine readers. It is more informative, a presentation of conditions hitherto but vaguely known, and at the same time it is an attempt to get at and into the heart and head of a little child.

And in this last analysis it would seem as if here existed the barrier insurmountable. It is much to be doubted if ever a genius will arise so thoughtful, so sensitive that he will penetrate into more than the merest outside integument of a child's heart. Certain phases have been guessed at with beautiful intention, certain rare insights have been attained with exquisite nicety, but somehow even the most sympathetic reader must feel that the insight is as rare as the interest is misguided.

Immanuel Kant conceived of, and, in the consummate power of his intellect, executed the " Critique of Pure Reason"; Darwin had taken the adult male and female human and tracked down their every emotion, impulse, quality and sentiment. The intellectual powers and heart-beats of a Napoleon or a Shakespeare have been reduced to more commonplace corner gossip, but after thousands of years of civilization, with the subject ever before us, its workings as near to us as air itself, the mind of a little child is as much a closed book, as much an enigma, as much a blank space upon the charts of our intellectual progress as at the very first.

Volumes have been written about the child, and stories for and of the child, and very learned men have lectured and other very eminent and noble men have taught, and it has all been going on for nineteen hundred and two years. And yet, notwithstanding all this, there lurks a mystery deep down within the eye of the five-year-old, a mystery that neither you nor I may know. You may see and understand what he actually does, but the thinking part of him is a second hidden nature that belongs to him and to other children, not to adults, not even to his mother. Once the older person invades the sphere of influence of this real undernature of the child and it congeals at once. It thaws and thrives only in the company of other children, and at the best we older ones may see it from a distance and from the outside. Between us and them it would appear that a great gulf is bridged; there is no knowing the child as he really is, and until the real child can be known the stories about him and the fiction and literature about him can at best be only a substitute for the real knowledge that probably never shall be ours.

NEWSPAPER CRITICISMS AND AMERICAN FICTION

NEWSPAPER CRITICISMS AND AMERICAN FICTION

THE limitations of space impose a restricted title, and one hastens to qualify the substantive "criticisms" by the adjective "average." Even "average" is not quite specialized enough; "vast majority" is more to the sense, and the proposition expanded to its fullest thus stands, "How is the vast majority of newspaper criticisms made, and how does it affect American Fiction?" And it may not be inappropriate at the outset to observe that one has adventured both hazards —criticism (of the "vast majority" kind) and also Fiction. One has criticized and has been criticized. Possibly then it may be permitted to speak a little authoritatively; not as the Scribes. Has it not astonished you how many of those things called by the new author "favourable reviews" may attach themselves —barnacles upon a lifeless hulk—to a novel that you know, that you know every one must, must know, is irretrievably bad? "On the whole, Mr. ——'s story is a capital bit of vigorous writing that we joyfully recommend"—

"A thrilling story palpitating with life," "One of the very best novels that has appeared in a long time," and the ever-new, ever-dutiful, ever-ready encomium, "Not a dull page in the book" (as if by the furthest stretch of conceivable human genius a book could be written that did not have a dull page; as if dull pages were not an absolute necessity). All these you may see strung after the announcement of publication of the novel. No matter, I repeat, how outrageously bad the novel may be. Now there is an explanation of this matter, and it is to be found not in the sincere admiration of little reviewers who lack the ingenuity to invent new phrases, but in the following fact: it is easier to write favourable than unfavourable reviews. It must be borne in mind that very few newspapers (comparatively) employ regularly paid book-reviewers whose business it is to criticize novels—and nothing else. Most book-reviewing is done as an odd job by sub-editors, assistants and special writers in the intervals between their regular work. They come to the task with a brain already jaded, an interest so low as to be almost negligible, and with—as often as not—a mind besieged by a thousand other cares, responsibilities and projects.

The chief has said something like this

(placing upon the scribe's table a column of novels easily four feet high, sent in for review):

"Say, B——, these things have been stacking up like the devil lately, and I don't want 'em kicking 'round the office any longer. Get through with them as quick as you can, and remember that in an hour there's such and such to be done."

I tell you I have seen it happen like this a hundred times. And the scribe " must " read and "review" between twenty and thirty books in an hour's time. One way of doing it is to search in the pages of the book for the "publisher's notice," a printed slip that has a favourable review—that is what it amounts to—all ready-made. The scribe merely turns this in with a word altered here and there. How he reviews the books that have not this publisher's notice Heaven only knows. He is not to blame, as they must be done in an hour. Twenty books in sixty minutes— three minutes to each book. Now, it is impossible to criticize a book adversely after a minute and a half of reading (we will allow a minute and a half for writing the review). In order to write unfavourably it is necessary to know what one is writing about. But it is astonishing how much commendatory palaver already exists that can be applied to any kind or condition of novel.   Is it a novel of adventure (the reviewer may know if it be such by the ship on the cover design)—it will be appropriate to use these terms: "Vibrant with energy," or "Full of fine fighting," or "The reader is carried with breathless interest from page to page of this exciting romance."   Is it a novel of rural life?   These may be made use of: "Replete with quaint humour," "A faithful picture of an interesting phase of American life," etc., etc.   Is it a story of the West (you can guess that from the chapter headings), it will be proper to say, "A strong and vital portraying of the wild life of the trail and frontier."

And so one might run through the entire list.   The books must be reviewed, the easiest way is the quickest, and the quickest way is to write in a mild and meaningless phraseology, innocuous, "favourable."   In this fashion is made the greater mass of American criticism. As to effects: It has of course no effect upon the novel's circulation.   Only one person is at all apt to take these reviews, this hack-work, seriously.

Only one person, I observed, is at all apt to take these reviews seriously.   This way lies the harm.   The new writer, the young fellow with his first book, who may not know the ways of reviewers.   The author, who collects these notices and pastes them in a scrap-book. He is perilously prone to believe what the hacks say, to believe that there is "no dull page in the story," that his novel is "one of the notable contributions to recent fiction," and cherishing this belief he is fated to a wrench and a heart-ache when, six months after publication day, the semi-annual account of copies sold is rendered. There is unfortunately no palaver in the writing of this—no mild-mannered phraseology; and the author is made to see suddenly that "this exciting romance" which the reviewers have said the readers "would follow with a breathless interest till the end is reached and then wish for more," has circulated among—possibly—five hundred of the breathless.

Thus, then, the vast majority of criticisms. It is not all, however, and it is only fair to say that there are exceptions—great papers which devote whole supplements to the consideration of literary matters and whose reviewers are deliberate, thoughtful fellows, who do not read more than one book a week, who sign their opinions and who have themselves a name, a reputation, to make or keep These must have an effect. But even the most conspicuous among them cannot influence very widely. They may help, so one believes, a good book which is already becoming popular.   No one of them can "make" a book by a ''favourable review,'' as they could a little while ago in France.   No number of them could do it, here in America. There are too many other reviewers.   No one man, nor aggregation of men, can monopolize the requisite authority.   And then with us the spirit of independent thinking and judgment is no doubt too prevalent.

NOVELISTS TO ORDER—WHILE YOU WAIT

NOVELISTS TO ORDER—WHILE YOU WAIT

NOT at all absurd, "Novelists to order— while you wait," provided you order the right sort, and are willing to wait long enough. In other words, it is quite possible to make a novelist, and a good one, too, if the thing is undertaken in the right spirit, just as it is possible to make a painter, or an actor, or a business man.

I am prepared to hear the old objections raised to this: "Ah, it must be born in you"; "no amount of training can 'make' an artist"; "poets are born and not made," etc., etc. But I am also willing to contend that a very large percentage of this talk is sheer non-sense, and that what the world calls "genius" is, as often as not, the results of average ability specialized and developed. The original "spark" in the child-mind, that later on "kindles the world into flame with its light," I do believe could be proved to be the same for the artist, the actor, the novelist, the inventor, even the financier and "magnate." It is only made to burn in different lamps. Nor does any one believe that this "spark" is any mysterious, supernatural gift, some marvelous, angelic "genius," God-given, Heaven-given, etc., etc., etc., but just plain, forthright, rectangular, everyday common sense, nothing more extraordinary or God-given than sanity. If it were true that Genius were the gift of the gods, it would also be true that hard work in cultivating it would be superfluous. As well be without genius if some plodder, some dullard, can by such work equal the best you can do—you with your God-given faculties.

Is it not much more reasonable—more noble, for the matter of that—to admit at once that all faculties, all intellects are God-given, the only difference being that some are specialized to one end, some to another, some not specialized at all. We call Rostand and Mr. Carnegie geniuses, but most of us would be unwilling to admit that the genius of the American financier differed in kind from the genius of the French dramatist. However, one believes that this is open to debate. As for my part, I suspect that, given a difference in environment and training, Rostand would have consolidated the American steel companies and Carnegie have written "L'Aiglon." But one dares to go a little further—a great deal further—and claims that the young Carnegie and the young Rostand were no more than intelligent, matter-of-fact boys, in no wise different from the common house variety, grammar school product. They have been trained differently, that is all.

Given the ordinarily intelligent ten-year-old, and, all things being equal, you can make anything you like out of him—a minister of the gospel or a green-goods man, an electrical engineer or a romantic poet, or—return to our muttons—a novelist. If a failure is the result, blame the method of training, not the quantity or quality of the ten-year-old's intellect. Don't say, if he is a failure as a fine novelist, that he lacks genius for writing, and would have been a fine business man. Make no mistake, if he did not have enough "genius" for novel-writing he would certainly have not had enough for business.

"Why, then," you will ask, "is it so impossible for some men, the majority of them, to write fine novels, or fine poems, or paint fine pictures? Why is it that this faculty seems to be reserved for the chosen few, the more refined, cultured, etc.? Why is it, in a word, that, for every artist (using the word to include writers, painters, actors, etc.) that appears there are thousands of business men, com·mercial "geniuses"?

The reason seems to lie in this: and it is

again a question of training. From the very first the average intelligent American boy is trained, not with a view toward an artistic career, but with a view to entering a business life. If the specialization of his faculties along artistic lines ever occurs at all it begins only when the boy is past the formative period. In other words, most people who eventually become artists are educated for the first eighteen or twenty years of their life along entirely unartistic lines. Biographies of artists are notoriously full of just such instances. The boy who is to become a business man finds, the moment he goes to school, a whole vast machinery of training made ready for his use, and not only is it a matter of education for him, but the whole scheme of modern civilization works in his behalf. No one ever heard of obstacles thrown in the way of the boy who announces for himself a money-making career; while for the artist, as is said, education, environment, the trend of civilization are not merely indifferent, but openly hostile and inimical. One hears only of those men who surmount—and at what cost to their artistic powers—those obstacles. How many thousands are there who succumb unrecorded!

So that it has not often been tried—the experiment of making a novelist while you wait—*i. e.*, taking a ten-year-old of average intelligence and training him to be a novelist. Suppose all this modern, this gigantic perfected machinery—all this resistless trend of a commercial civilization were set in motion in favour of the little aspirant for honours in artistic fields, who is to say with such a training he would not in the end be a successful artist, painter, poet, musician or novelist. Training, not "genius," would make him.

Then, too, another point. The artistic training should begin much, much earlier than the commercial training—instead of, as at present, so much later.

Nowadays, as a rule, the artist's training begins, as was said, after a fourth of his life, the very best, the most important has been lived. You can take a boy of eighteen and make a business man of him in ten years. But at eighteen the faculties that make a good artist are very apt to be atrophied, hardened, unworkable. Even the ten-year-old is almost too old to begin on. The first ten years of childhood are the imaginative years, the creative years, the observant years, the years of a fresh interest in life. The child "imagines" terrors or delights, ghosts or fairies, creates a world out of his toys, and observes to an extent that adults have no idea of. ("Give me," a detective once told me, "a child's description of a man that is wanted. It beats an adult's every single time.") And imagination, creation, observation and an unblunted interest in life are exactly the faculties most needed by novelists.

At eighteen there comes sophistication—or a pretended sophistication, which is deadlier. Other men's books take the place of imagination for the young man; creation in him is satisfied by dramas, horse-races and amusements. The newspapers are his observation, and oh, how he assumes to be above any pleasure in simple, vigorous life!

So that at eighteen it is, as a rule, too late to make a fine novelist out of him. He may start out in that career, but he will not go far—so far as he would in business. But if he was taken in hand as soon as he could write in words of three syllables, and instead of being crammed with commercial arithmetic (How many marbles did A have? If a man buys a piece of goods at $12\frac{1}{2}$ cents and sells it for 15 cents, etc., etc.)—

If he had been taken in hand when his imagination was alive, his creative power vigorous, his observation lynxlike, and his interest keen, and trained with a view toward the production of original fiction, who is to say how far he would have gone?

One does not claim that the artist is above the business man. Far from it. Only, when you have choked the powers of imagination and observation, and killed off the creative ability, and deadened the interest in life, don't call it lack of genius.

Nor when some man of a different race than ours, living in a more congenial civilization, whose training from his youth up has been adapted to a future artistic profession, succeeds in painting the great picture, composing the great prelude, writing the great novel, don't say he was born a "genius," but rather admit that he was made "to order" by a system whose promoters knew how to wait.

THE "NATURE" REVIVAL IN
LITERATURE

THE "NATURE" REVIVAL IN LITER-
ATURE

IT has been a decade of fads, and ''the people have imagined a vain thing," as they have done from the time of Solomon and as no doubt they will till the day of the New Jerusalem. And in no other line of activity has the instability and changeableness of the taste of the public been so marked as in that of literature. Such an overturning of old gods and such a setting up of new ones, such an image-breaking, shrine-smashing, relic-ripping carnival I doubt has ever been witnessed in all the history of writing. It has been a sort of literary Declaration of Independence. For half a century certain great names, from Irving down to Holmes, were veritable *Abra-cadabras*—impeccable, sanctified. Then all at once the *fin de siecle* irreverence seemed to invade all sorts and conditions simultaneously, and the somber, sober idols were shouldered off into the dark niches, and not a man of us that did not trundle forth his own little tin-god-on-wheels, kowtowing and making obeisance, and going before with cymbals and a great noise, proclaiming a New Great One; now it was the great Colonial Image, now the Great Romantic Image, now the Great Minor-German Kingdom Image.

There are a great many very eminent and very wise critics who frown upon and deplore the reaction. But it is a question if, after all, the movement will not prove—ultimately—beneficial. Convention, blind adherence to established forms, inertia, is the dry rot of a national literature. Better the American public should read bad books than no books, and that same public is reading now as never before. It is a veritable upheaval, a breaking-up of all the old grounds. Better this than supineness; better this than immobility. Once the ground turned over a bit, harrowed and loosened, and the place is made ready for the good seed.

Some of this, one chooses to believe, has already been implanted. In all the parade of the new little tin-gods some may be discovered that are not tin, but sterling. Of all the fads, the most legitimate, the most abiding, the most inherent—so it would appear—is the "Nature" revival. Indeed, it is not fair to call it a fad at all. For it is a return to the primitive, sane life of the country, and the natural thing by its very character cannot be artificial, cannot be a "fad." The writers who have followed where Mr. Thompson Seton blazed the way are so numerous and so well known that it is almost superfluous in this place to catalogue or criticize them. But it is significant of the strength of this movement that such an outdoor book as "Bob, Son of Battle," was unsuccessful in England, and only attained its merited popularity when published here in America. We claimed the "good gray dog" as our own from the very first, recognizing that the dog has no nationality, being indeed a citizen of the whole world. The flowers in "Elizabeth's German Garden"—also world citizens—we promptly transplanted to our own soil. Mr. Mowbray, with his mingling of fact and fiction, made his country home for the benefit—I have no doubt—of hundreds who have actually worked out the idea suggested in his pages. The butterfly books, the garden books, the flower books, expensive as they are, have been in as much demand as some very popular novels. Mr. Dugmore astonished and delighted a surprisingly large public with his marvelous life-photographs of birds, while even President Roosevelt himself deemed Mr. Wallihan's "Photographs of Big Game" of so much importance and value that he wrote the introductory notice to that excellent volume.

It is hardly possible to pick up a magazine now that does not contain the story of some animal hero. Time was when we relegated this sort to the juvenile periodicals. But now we cannot get too much of it. Wolves, rabbits, hounds, foxes, the birds, even the reptilia, all are dramatized, all figure in their little rôles. Tobo and the Sand-hill Stag parade upon the same pages as Mr. Christie's *debutantes* and Mr. Smedley's business men, and, if you please, have their love affairs and business in precisely the same spirit. All this cannot but be significant, and, let us be assured, significant of good. The New England school for too long dominated the entire range of American fiction— limiting it, specializing it, polishing, refining and embellishing it, narrowing it down to a veritable cult, a thing to be safeguarded by the elect, the few, the aristocracy. It is small wonder that the reaction came when and as it did; small wonder that the wearied public, roused at length, smashed its idols with such vehemence; small wonder that, declaring its independence and finding itself suddenly untrammeled and unguided, it flew off "*mobishly*" toward false gods, good only because they were new.

All this is small wonder. The great wonder is this return to nature, this unerring groping backward toward the fundamentals, in order to take a renewed grip upon life. If you care to see a proof of how vital it is, how valuable, look into some of the magazines of the seventies and eighties. It is astonishing to consider that we ever found an interest in them. The effect is like entering a darkened room. And not only the magazines, but the entire literature of the years before the nineties is shadowed and oppressed with the bugbear of "literature." Outdoor life was a thing apart from our reading. Even the tales and serials whose *mise en scene* was in the country had no breath of the country in them. The "literature" in them suffocated the life, and the humans with their everlasting consciences, their heated and artificial activities, filled all the horizon, admitting the larks and the robins only as accessories; considering the foxes, the deer and the rabbits only as creatures to be killed, to be pursued, to be exterminated. But Mr. Seton and his school, and the Mowbrays, and the Ollivants, the Dugmores and the Wallihans opened a door, opened a window, and mere literature has had to give place to life. The sun has come in and the great winds, and the smell of the baking alkali on the Arizona deserts and the reek of the tar-weed on the Colorado slopes; and nature has ceased to exist as a classification of science, has ceased to be *mis*-understood as an aggregate of botany, zoölogy, geology and the like, and has become a thing intimate and familiar and rejuvenating.

There is no doubt that the estate of American letters is experiencing a renaissance. Formality, the old idols, the demi-gorgons and autocrats no longer hold an absolute authority. A multitude of false gods are clamouring for recognition, shouldering one another about to make room for their altars, soliciting incense as if it were patronage. No doubt these "draw many after them," but the "nature revival" has brought the galvanizing, vital element into this tumult of little inkling sham divinities and has shown that life is better than "literature," even if the "literature" be of human beings and the life be that of a faithful dog.

Vitality is the thing, after all. Dress the human puppet never so gaily, bedeck it never so brilliantly, pipe before it never so cunningly, and, fashioned in the image of God though it be, just so long as it is a puppet and not a person, just so long the great heart of the people will turn from it, in weariness and disgust, to find its interest in the fidelity of

the sheep-dog of the North o' England, the
intelligence of a prairie wolf of Colorado, or
the death-fight of a bull moose in the tim-
berlands of Ontario.

THE MECHANICS OF FICTION

THE MECHANICS OF FICTION

WE approach a delicate subject. And if the manner of approach is too serious it will be very like the forty thousand men of the King of France who marched terribly and with banners to the top of the hill with the meager achievement of simply getting there. Of all the arts, as one has previously observed, that of novel-writing is the least mechanical. Perhaps, after all, rightly so; still it is hard to escape some formality, some forms. There must always be chapter divisions, also a beginning and an end, which implies a middle, continuity, which implies movement, which in turn implies a greater speed or less, an accelerated, retarded or broken action; and before the scoffer is well aware he is admitting a multitude of set forms. No one who sets a thing in motion but keeps an eye and a hand upon its speed. No one who constructs but keeps watch upon the building, strengthening here, lightening there, here at the foundations cautious and conservative, there at the cornice fantastic and daring. In all human occupations, trades, arts or business, science, morals

147

or religion, there exists, way at the bottom, a homogeneity and a certain family likeness, so that, quite possibly after all, the discussion of the importance of the mechanics of fiction may be something more than mere speculative sophistry.

A novel addresses itself primarily to a reader, and it has been so indisputably established that the reader's time and effort of attention must be economized that the fact need not be mentioned in this place—it would not economize the reader's time nor effort of attention.

Remains then the means to be considered, or in other words, How best to tell your story.

It depends naturally upon the nature of the story. The formula which would apply to one would not be appropriate for another. That is very true, but at the same time it is hard to get away from that thing in any novel which, let us call, the pivotal event. All good novels have one. It is the peg upon which the fabric of the thing hangs, the nucleus around which the shifting drifts and currents must—suddenly —coagulate, the sudden releasing of the brake to permit for one instant the entire machinery to labour, full steam, ahead. Up to that point the action must lead; from it, it must decline.

But—and here one holds at least one mechanical problem—the approach, the leading up to this pivotal event must be infinitely slower than the decline. For the reader's interest in the story centres around it, and once it is disposed of attention is apt to dwindle very rapidly—and thus back we go again to the economy proposition.

It is the slow approach, however, that tells. The unskilled, impatient of the tedium of meticulous elaboration, will rush at it in a furious gallop of short chapters and hurried episodes, so that he may come the sooner to the purple prose declamation and drama that he is sure he can handle with such tremendous effect.

Not so the masters. Watch them during the first third—say—of their novels. Nothing happens—or at least so you fancy. People come and go, plans are described, localities, neighbourhoods; an incident crops up just for a second for which you can see no reason, a note sounds that is puzzlingly inappropriate. The novel continues. There seems to be no progress; again that perplexing note, but a little less perplexing. By now we are well into the story. There are no more new people, but the old ones come back again and again, and yet again; you remember them now after they are off the stage; you are more intimate with the two main characters.   Then comes a series of pretty incidents in which these two are prominent.   The action still lags, but little by little you are getting more and more acquainted with these principal actors.   Then perhaps comes the first acceleration of movement.   The approach begins—ever so little—to rise, and that same note which seemed at first so out of tune sounds again and this time drops into place in the progression, beautifully harmonious, correlating the whole gamut.   By now all the people are "on"; by now all the groundwork is prepared.   You know the localities so well that you could find your way about among them in the dark; hero and heroine are intimate acquaintances.

Now the action begins to increase in speed. The complication suddenly tightens; all along the line there runs a sudden alert.   An episode far back there in the first chapter, an episode with its appropriate group of characters, is brought forward and, coming suddenly to the front, collides with the main line of development and sends it off upon an entirely unlooked-for tangent.   Another episode of the second chapter—let us suppose—all at once makes common cause with a more recent incident, and the two produce a wholly unlooked-for counter-influence which swerves the main theme in still another direction, and all this time the action is speeding faster and faster, the complication tightening and straining to the breaking point, and then at last a "motif" that has been in preparation ever since the first paragraph of the first chapter of the novel suddenly comes to a head, and in a twinkling the complication is solved with all the violence of an explosion, and the catastrophe, the climax, the pivotal event fairly leaps from the pages with a rush of action that leaves you stunned, breathless and overwhelmed with the sheer power of its presentation. And there is a master-work of fiction.

Reading, as the uninitiated do, without an eye to the mechanics, without a consciousness of the wires and wheels and cogs and springs of the affair, it seems inexplicable that these great scenes of fiction—short as they are— some of them less than a thousand words in length—should produce so tremendous an effect by such few words, such simple language; and that sorely overtaxed word, "genius," is made to do duty as the explanation. But the genius is rare that in one thousand simple words, taken by themselves, could achieve the effect— for instance—of the fight aboard *The Flying Scud* in Stevenson's "Wrecker." Taken by itself, the scene is hardly important except from the point of view of style and felicity of expression. It is the context of the story that makes it so tremendous, and because Osborne and Stevenson prepared for that very scene from the novel's initial chapter.

And it seems as if there in a phrase one could resume the whole system of fiction-mechanics— preparations of effect.

The unskilled will invariably attempt to atone for lack of such painstaking preparation for their "Grande Scenes" by hysteria, and by exclamation in presenting the catastrophe. They declaim, they shout, stamp, shake their fists and flood the page with sonorous adjectives, call upon heaven and upon God. They summon to their aid every broken-down device to rouse the flaccid interest of the reader, and conclusively, irretrievably and ignominiously fail. It is too late for heroic effort then, and the reader, uninterested in the character, unfamiliar with the *locale*, unattracted by any charm of "atmosphere," lays down the book unperturbed and forgets it before dinner.

Where is the fault? Is it not in defective machinery? The analogies are multitudinous. The liner with hastily constructed boilers will flounder when she comes to essay the storm; and no stoking however vigorous, no oiling however eager, if delayed till then, will avail to aid her to ride through successfully. It is not the time to strengthen a wall when the hurricane threatens; prop and stay will not brace it then. Then the thing that tells is the plodding, slow, patient, brick-by-brick work, that only half shows down there at the foot half-hidden in the grass, obscure, unnoted. No genius is necessary for this sort of work, only great patience and a willingness to plod, for the time being.

No one is expected to strike off the whole novel in one continued fine frenzy of inspiration. As well expect the stone-mason to plant his wall in a single day. Nor is it possible to lay down any rule of thumb, any hard-and-fast schedule in the matter of novel writing. But no work is so ephemeral, so delicate, so—in a word—artistic that it cannot be improved by systematizing.

There is at least one indisputably good manner in which the unskilled may order his work—besides the one of preparation already mentioned. He may consider each chapter as a unit, distinct, separate, having a definite beginning, rise, height and end, the action continuous, containing no break in time, the locality unchanged throughout—no shifting of the scene to another environment. Each chapter thus treated is a little work in itself,

and the great story of the whole novel is told
thus as it were in a series of pictures, the author
supplying information as to what has inter-
vened between the end of one chapter and the
beginning of the next by suggestion or by
actual *resume*. As often as not the reader
himself can fill up the gap by the context.

This may be over-artificial, and it is conceivable that there are times when it is necessary to throw artificiality to the winds. But
it is the method that many of the greatest
fiction writers have employed, and even a
defective system is—at any rate, in fiction—
better than none.

FICTION WRITING AS A
BUSINESS

FICTION WRITING AS A BUSINESS

THE exaggerated and exalted ideas of the unenlightened upon this subject are, I have found, beyond all reason and beyond all belief. The superstition that with the publication of the first book comes fame and affluence is as firmly rooted as that other delusion which asks us to suppose that "a picture in the Paris Salon" is the certificate of success, ultimate, final, definite.

One knows, of course, that very naturally the "Eben Holden" and "David Harum" and "Richard Carvel" fellows make fortunes, and that these are out of the discussion; but also one chooses to assume that the average, honest, middle-class author supports himself and even a family by the sale of his novels—lives on his royalties.

Royalties! Why in the name of heaven were they called that, those microscopic sums that too, too often are less royal than beggarly? It has a fine sound—royalty. It fills the mouth. It can be said with an air—royalty. But there are plenty of these same royalties that will not pay the typewriter's bill.

157

Take an average case. No, that will not do, either, for the average published novel—I say it with my right hand raised—is, irretrievably, hopelessly and conclusively, a financial failure.

Take, then, an unusually lucky instance, literally a novel whose success is extraordinary, a novel which has sold 2,500 copies. I repeat that this is an extraordinary success. Not one book out of fifteen will do as well. But let us consider it. The author has worked upon it for—at the very least—three months. It is published. Twenty-five hundred copies are sold. Then the sale stops. And by the word stop one means cessation in the completest sense of the word. There are people—I know plenty of them—who suppose that when a book is spoken of as having stopped selling, a generality is intended, that merely a falling off of the initial demand has occurred. Error. When a book—a novel—stops selling, it stops with the definiteness of an engine when the fire goes out. It stops with a suddenness that is appalling, and thereafter not a copy, not one single, solitary copy is sold. And do not for an instant suppose that ever after the interest may be revived. A dead book can no more be resuscitated than a dead dog.

But to go back. The 2,500 have been sold.

The extraordinary, the marvelous has been achieved. What does the author get out of it? A royalty of ten per cent. Two hundred and fifty dollars for three months' hard work. Roughly, less than $20 a week, a little more than $2.50 a day. An expert carpenter will easily make twice that, and the carpenter has infinitely the best of it in that he can keep the work up year in and year out, where the novelist must wait for a new idea, and the novel writer must then jockey and maneuver for publication. Two novels a year is about as much as the writer can turn out and yet keep a marketable standard. Even admitting that both the novels sell 2,500 copies, there is only $500 of profit. In the same time the carpenter has made his $1,800, nearly four times as much. One may well ask the question: Is fiction writing a money-making profession?

The astonishing thing about the affair is that a novel may make a veritable stir, almost a sensation, and yet fail to sell very largely.

There is so-and-so's book. Everywhere you go you hear about it. Your friends have read it. It is in demand at the libraries. You don't pick up a paper that does not contain a review of the story in question. It is in the "Book of the Month" column. It is even, even—the pinnacle of achievement—in that shining roster, the list of best sellers of the week.

Why, of course the author is growing rich! Ah, at last he has arrived! No doubt he will build a country house out of his royalties. Lucky fellow; one envies him.

Catch him unawares and what is he doing? As like as not writing unsigned book reviews at five dollars a week in order to pay his board bill—and glad of the chance.

It seems incredible. But one must remember this: That for every one person who buys a book, there will be six who will talk about it. And the half-thousand odd reviewers who are writing of the book do not buy it, but receive "editorial" copies from the publishers, upon which no royalty is paid.

I know it for an undisputed fact that a certain novel which has ever been called the best American novel of the nineteenth century, and which upon publication was talked about, written about and even preached about, from the Atlantic to the Pacific, took ten years in which to attain the sale of 10,000 copies. Even so famous, so brilliant an author as Harold Frederic did not at first sell conspicuously. "That Lawton Girl," "The Copperhead," "Seth's Brother's Wife," masterpieces though they are, never made money for the writer.

Each sold about 2,000 copies. Not until "Theron Ware" was published did Mr. Frederic reap his reward.

Even so great a name as that of George Meredith is not a "sesame," and only within the last few years has the author of "Evan Harrington" made more than five or six hundred dollars out of any one of his world-famous books.

But of course there is another side. For one thing, the author is put to no expense in the composing of his novel. (It is not always necessary to typewrite the manuscript.) The carpenter must invest much money in tools; must have a shop. Shop rent and tools repaired or replaced cut into his $1,800 of profit. Or take it in the fine arts. The painter must have a studio, canvases, models, brushes, a whole equipment; the architect must have his draughting room, the musician his instrument. But so far as initial expense is concerned, a half-dollar will buy every conceivable necessary tool the novelist may demand. He needs no office, shop or studio; models are not required. The libraries of the city offer him a quiet working place if the home is out of the question. Nor, as one has so often urged, is any expensive training necessary before his money-earning capacity is attained. The architect must buy instruction for many years. The painter must study in expensive studios, the musician must learn in costly conservatories, the singer must be taught by high-priced maestros. Furthermore, it is often necessary for the aspirant to travel great distances to reach the cities where his education is to be furthered; almost invariably a trip to and a residence in Europe is indispensable. It is a great undertaking and an expensive one to prepare for the professions named, and it takes years of time—years during which the aspirant is absolutely non-productive.

But the would-be novel writer may determine between breakfast and dinner to essay the plunge, buy (for a few cents) ink and paper between dinner and supper, and have the novel under way before bedtime.

How much of an outlay of money does his first marketable novel represent? Practically nothing. On the other hand, let us ask the same question of, say, the painter. How much money has he had to spend before he was able to paint his first marketable picture? To reach a total sum he must foot up the expenses of at least five years of instruction and study, the cost of living during that time, the cost of materials, perhaps even the price of a trip to Paris. Easily the sum may reach $5,000.

Fifty cents' worth of ink and paper do not loom large beside this figure.

Then there are other ways in which the fiction writer may earn money—by fiction. The novelist may look down upon the mere writer of short stories, or may even look down upon himself in the same capacity, but as a rule the writer of short stories is the man who has the money. It is much easier to sell the average short story than the average novel. Infinitely easier. And the short story of the usual length will fetch $100. One thousand people—think of it—one thousand people must buy copies of your novel before it will earn so much for you. It takes three months to complete the novel— the novel that earns the $250. But with ingenuity, the writer should be able to turn out six short stories in the same time, and if he has luck in placing them there is $600 earned—more than twice the sum made by the novel. So that the novelist may eke out the alarming brevity of his semiannual statements by writing and selling "short stuff."

Then—so far as the novel is concerned— there is one compensation, one source of revenue which the writer enjoys and which is, as a rule, closed to all others. Once the carpenter sells his piece of work it is sold for good and all. The painter has but one chance to make money

from the sale of his picture. The architect
receives payment for his design and there is the
end.   But the novelist—and one speaks now of
the American—may sell the same work over
many times.   Of course, if the novel is a failure it is a failure, and no more is said.   But
suppose it is a salable, readable, brisk bit of
narrative, with a swift action and rapid movement.   Properly managed, this, under favourable conditions, might be its life history:
First it is serialized either in the Sunday press
or, less probably, in a weekly or monthly.
Then it is made up into book form and sent over
the course a second time.   The original publisher sells sheets to a Toronto or Montreal
house and a Canadian edition reaps a like
harvest.   It is not at all unlikely that a special
cheap cloth edition may be bought and launched
by some large retailer either of New York or
Chicago.   Then comes the paper edition—with
small royalties, it is true, but based upon an
enormous number of copies, for the usual paper
edition is an affair of tens of thousands.   Next
the novel crosses the Atlantic and a small sale
in England helps to swell the net returns, which
again are added to—possibly—by the "colonial
edition" which the English firm issues.   Last
of all comes the Tauchnitz edition, and with
this (bar the improbable issuing of later special

editions) the exploitation ceases. Eight separate times the same commodity has been sold, no one of the sales militating against the success of the other seven, the author getting his fair slice every time. Can any other trade, profession or art (excepting only the dramatist, which is, after all, a sister art) show the like? Even (speaking of the dramatist) there may be a ninth reincarnation of the same story and the creatures of the writer's pages stalk forth upon the boards in cloak and buskin.

And there are the indirect ways in which he may earn money. Some of his ilk there are who lecture. Nor are there found wanting those who read from their own works. Some write editorials or special articles in the magazines and newspapers with literary departments. But few of them have "princely" incomes.

THE "VOLUNTEER MANU-
SCRIPT"

THE "VOLUNTEER MANUSCRIPT"

AT a conservative estimate there are 70,000,000 people in the United States. At a liberal estimate 100,000 of these have lost the use of both arms; remain then 69,900,000 who write novels. Indeed, many are called, but few—oh, what a scanty, skimped handful that few represent—are chosen.

The work of choosing these few, or rather of rejecting these many, devolves upon the manuscript readers for the baker's dozen of important New York publishing houses, and a strange work it is, and strange are the contributions that pass under their inspection.

As one not unfamiliar with the work of "reading," the present writer may offer a little seasonable advice.

1. First have your manuscript typewritten. The number of manuscripts is too great and the time too short to expect the reader to decipher script; and, besides, ideas presented or scenes described in type are infinitely more persuasive, more plausible than those set down in script. A good story typewritten will appear

to better advantage; a poor one similarly treated seems less poverty stricken.

2. Do not, by any manner of means, announce in a prefatory note that you "lay no claim to literary excellence," with the intention thereby of ingratiating yourself with regard to the "reader," winning him over by a parade of modesty.   Invariably the statement is prejudicial, producing an effect exactly contrary to the one desired.   It will make the mildest of "readers" angry.   If you have no claims upon literary excellence, why in Heaven's name are you bothering him to read your work?

3. Enclose a forwarding address in case of rejection.   This, seemingly, is superfluous advice.   But it is astonishing how many manuscripts come in innocent even of the author's name, with never a scrap nor clue as to their proper destination.

4. Don't ask for criticism.   The reader is not a critic.   He passes only upon the availability of the manuscript for the uses of the publisher who employs him.   And a manuscript of paramount literary quality may be rejected for any number of reasons, none of which have anything to do with its literary worth—or accepted for causes equally outside the domain of letters.   Criticism is one thing, professional "reading" quite another.

5. Don't bother about "enclosing stamps for return." The manuscript will go back to you by c. o. d. express.

6. Don't submit a part of a manuscript. It is hard enough sometimes to judge the story as a whole, and no matter how discouraging the initial chapter may be the publisher will always ask to see the remaining portions before deciding.

7. Don't write to the publisher beforehand asking him if he will consider your manuscript. If it is a novel he will invariably express his willingness to consider it. How can he tell whether he wants it or not until he, through his "reader," has seen it?

8. Don't expect to get an answer much before a month. Especially if your story has merit, it must pass through many hands and be considered by many persons before judgment is rendered. The better it is the longer you will wait before getting a report.

9. Don't, in Heaven's name, enclose commendatory letters written by your friends, favourable reviews by your pastor or by the president of the local college. The story will speak for itself more distinctly than any of your acquaintances.

10. Don't say you will revise or shorten to suit the tastes or judgment of the publisher.

At best that's a servile humility that in itself is a confession of weakness and that will make you no friends at court.

11. Don't forward a letter of introduction, no matter from how near a friend of the publisher. The publisher will only turn the MS. over to his "readers," and with them the letter from a stranger carries no weight.

12. Don't write a Colonial novel.

13. Don't write a Down East novel.

14. Don't write a "Prisoner of Zenda" novel.

15. Don't write a novel.

16. Try to keep your friends from writing novels.

And of all the rules, one is almost tempted to declare that the last two are the most important. For to any one genuinely interested in finding "good stuff" in the ruck and run of volunteer manuscripts, nothing is more discouraging, nothing more apparently hopeless of ultimate success than the consistent and uniform trashiness of the day's batch of submitted embryonic novels. Infinitely better for their author had they never been written; infinitely better for him had he employed his labour—at the very least it is labour of three months—upon the trade or profession to which he was bred. It is very hard work to write a good novel, but it is much harder to write a bad one. Its very infelicity is a snare to the pen, its very clumsiness a constant demand for laborious boosting and propping.

And consider another and further word of advice—number 17, if you please. Don't go away with that popular idea that your manuscript will be considered, or if really and undeniably good will be heedlessly rejected. Bad manuscripts are not read from cover to cover. The reader has not the right to waste his employer's time in such unremunerative diligence. Often a page or two will betray the hopelessness of the subsequent chapters, and no one will demand of the "reader" a perusal of a work that he knows will be declined in the end.

Nor was there ever a sincere and earnest effort that went unappreciated in a publisher's place of business. I have seen an entire office turned upside down by a "reader" who believed he had discovered among the batch of voluminous MS. something "really good, you know," and who almost forced a reading of the offering in question upon every member of the firm from the senior partner down to the assistant salesman.

As a rule, all manuscripts follow the same routine. From the clerk who receives them at the hands of the expressman they go to the recorder, who notes the title, address and date of arrival, and also, after turning them over to the junior reader, the fact of the transfer. The junior reader's report upon the manuscript is turned in to one of the members of the firm, whose decision is final. The manuscript itself goes up to the senior reader, who also reports upon it to the firm member. If both reports are unfavourable, this latter directs the manuscript to be returned with or without a personal letter, as he deems proper. If both the readers' reports are favourable, or even if one is sufficiently laudatory, he calls for the manuscript and reads it himself. If he disagrees with the readers' reports, the manuscript is declined. If not, he passes the manuscript on to one of the partners of the house, who also reads it. The two "talk it over," and out of the conference comes the ultimate decision in the matter.

Sometimes the circulation manager and head salesman are consulted to decide whether or not—putting all questions of the book's literary merits aside—the "thing will sell." And doubt not for a moment that their counsel carries weight.

Another feature of the business which it is very well to remember is that all publishers cannot be held responsible for the loss of or damage to unsolicited manuscripts. If you submit the MS. of a novel you do it at your own risk, and the carelessness of an office-boy may lose for you the work of many months—years, even; work that you could never do over again. You could demand legally no reparation. The publishers are not responsible. Only in a case where a letter signed by one of the "heads" has been sent to the author requesting that the manuscript be forwarded does the situation become complicated. But in the case of an unknown writer the monetary value of his work in a court of law would be extremely difficult to place, and even if an award of damages could be extorted it would hardly more than pay the typewriter's bill.

But the loss of manuscript may be of serious import to the publisher for all that. That reputation for negligence in the matter of handling unsolicited matter fastens upon a firm with amazing rapidity. Bothersome as the number of volunteer manuscripts are, they do—to a certain extent—gauge the importance of a given concern. And as they arrive in constantly increasing quantities, the house may know that it is growing in favour and in reputation: and so a marked falling off reverses the situation. Writers will be naturally averse to submitting manuscripts to offices which are known to be careless. And I know of at least one instance where the loss of a couple of manuscripts within a month produced a marked effect upon the influx of the volunteers. Somehow the news of the loss always gets out, and spreads by some mysterious means till it is heard of from strangely remote quarters. The author will, of course, tell his friends of the calamity, and will make more ado over the matter than if his story was accepted. Of course, this particular story is the one great masterpiece of his career; the crass stupidity of the proud and haughty publisher has ruined his chance of success, and the warning: "Don't send your stuff to that firm.   It will be lost!" is passed on all along the line.   So that repeated instances of the negligence may in the end embarrass the publisher, and the real masterpiece, the first novel of a New Man, goes to a rival.

I have in mind one case where a manuscript was lost under peculiarly distressing circumstances. The reader, who had his office in the editorial rooms of a certain important house of New York, was on a certain day called to the reception room to interview one of the host of writers who came daily to submit their offerings in person.

In this case the reader confronted a little gentleman in the transition period of genteel decay. He was a Frenchman. His mustache, tight, trim and waxed, was white. The frock coat was buttoned only at the waist; a silk handkerchief puffed from the pocket, and a dried carnation, lamentably faded, that had done duty for many days, enlivened with a feeble effort the worn silk lapel.

But the innate French effervescence, debonair, *insouciant*, was not gone yet. The little gentleman presented a card. Of course the name boasted that humblest of titles— baron. The Baron, it appeared, propitiated destiny by "Instruction in French, German and Italian," but now instruction was no longer propitious. With a deprecating giggle this was explained; the Baron did not wish to make the "reader" feel bad—to embarrass him.

"I will probably starve very soon," he observed, still with the modifying little giggle, and, of course, the inevitable shrug, "unless— my faith—something turns up."

It was to be turned up, evidently, by means of an attenuated manuscript which he presented. He had written—during the intervals of instruction—a series of articles on the character of Americans as seen by a Frenchman, and these had been published by a newspaper of the town in which he instructed—an absolutely obscure town, lost and forgotten, away up among the New Hampshire hills.

The articles, he insinuated, might be made into a book—a book that might be interesting to the great American public. And, with a *naivete* that was absolutely staggering, he assumed without question that the firm would publish his book—that it was really an important contribution to American literature.

He would admit that he had not been paid very liberally by the country paper for the articles as they appeared. He was not Emile Zola. If he was he might have sold his articles at fifteen or twenty dollars each.

He said just that. Think of it! The poor little Instructor-Baron Zola! Fifteen dollars! Well!

He left the articles—neatly cut out and pasted in a copy-book—with the "reader," and gave as his address a dreadfully obscure hotel.

The "reader" could not make up his mouth to tell him, even before looking over the first paragraph of the first article, that as a book the commercial value of the offering was absolutely, irrevocably and hopelessly nil, and so the little manuscript went into the mill—and in two days was lost.

I suppose that never in the history of that particular firm was the search for a missing

manuscript prosecuted with half the energy
or ardour that ensued upon the discovery of
this particular loss. From the desk-files of
the senior partner to the shipping-slips of the
packer's assistant the hunt proceeded—and all
in vain.

Meanwhile the day approached on which the
Baron was to come for his answer and at last it
arrived, and promptly at the appointed hour
the poor little card with the hyphenated titled
name written carefully and with beautiful
flourishes in diluted ink was handed in.

Do you know what the publisher did? He
wrote the absurd, pompous name across the
order line of a check and signed his own name
underneath, and the check was for an amount
that would make even unpropitious Destiny
take off his hat and bow politely.

And I tell you that my little Instructor-
Baron, with eminent good-humour, but with the
grand manner, a *Marechal du royaume*, waved
it aside. Turenne could have been no more
magnificent. (They do order these matters
better in France.) His whole concern—
hunger-pinched as he may easily have been
at the very moment—his whole concern was
to put the embarrassed publisher at his ease,
to make this difficulty less difficult.

He assured him that his articles were written

comme-ci, comme-ca, for his own amusement, that he could not think of accepting, etc.

And I like to remember that this whole affair, just as if it had been prepared in advance for a popular magazine whose editor insisted upon "happy endings," did end well, and the publisher, who at the moment was involved in the intricacies of a vast correspondence with a Parisian publishing house, found a small position as translator in one of his sub-departments for the little Instructor-Baron who had the great good fortune to suffer the loss of a manuscript—in the right place.

And now the card—engraved, if you please—bears proudly the Baron's name, supported by the inscription, "Official Translator and Director of Foreign Correspondence to the Firm of —— & Co., Publishers."

RETAIL BOOKSELLER: LITERARY DICTATOR

RETAIL BOOKSELLER: LITERARY DICTATOR

O F all the various and different kinds and characters of people who are concerned in the writing and making of a novel, including the author, the publisher, the critic, the salesman, the advertisement writer, the drummer—of all this "array of talent," as the bill-boards put it, which one has the most influence in the success of the book? Who, of all these, can, if he chooses, help or hurt the sales the most?—assuming for the moment that sales are the index of success, the kind of success that at the instant we are interested in.

Each one of these people has his followers and champions. There are not found wanting those who say the publisher is the all-in-all. And again it is said that a critic of authority can make a book by a good review or ruin it by an unfavourable one. The salesman, others will tell you—he who is closest allied to the money transaction—can exert the all-powerful influence. Or again, surely in this day of exploitation and publicity the man who concocts great "ads" is the important one.

The author is next included. He can do no more than write the book, and as good books have failed and bad ones have succeeded— always considering failure and success in their most sordid meanings—the mere writing need not figure. But the fact remains that there are cases where publishers have exerted every device to start a book and still have known it to remain upon their hands; that critics have raved to heaven or damned to hell, and the novel has fallen or flown in spite and not because of them; that salesmen have cajoled and schemed, and yet have returned with unfilled orders, and that advertisements that have clamoured so loudly that even they who ran must have read, and yet the novel in question remained inert, immovable, a failure, a "plug."

All these, then, have been tried and at times have been found wanting. There yet remains one exponent of the business of distributing fiction who has not been considered. He, one claims, can do more than any or all of the gentlemen just mentioned to launch or strand a novel.

Now let it be understood that by no possible manner of means does one consider him infallible. Again and again have his best efforts come to nothing. This, however, is what is claimed: he has more influence on success or failure than any of the others. And who is he?

The retailer. One can almost affirm that he is a determining factor in American fiction; that, in a limited sense, with him, his is the future. Author, critic, analyst and essayist may hug to themselves a delusive phantom of hope that they are the moulders of public opinion, they and they alone. That may be, sometimes. But consider the toiling and spinning retailer. What does the failure or success of the novel mean to the critic? Nothing more than a minute and indefinite increase or decrease of prestige. The publisher who has many books upon his list may recoup himself on one failure by a compensating success. The salesman's pay goes on just the same whether his order slips are full or blank; likewise the stipend of the writer of "ads." The author has no more to lose—materially—than the price of ink and paper. But to the retail bookseller a success means money made; failure, money lost. If he can dispose of an order of fifty books he is ahead by calculable, definite, concrete profits. If he cannot dispose of the fifty his loss is equally calculable, equally definite, equally concrete. Naturally, being a business man, he is a cautious man. He will not order a book which he deems unsalable, but he will lay in a stock of one that promises returns. Through him the book is distributed to the public. If he has a book in stock, the public gets it. If he does not have it, the public goes without. The verdict of the public is the essential to popularity or unpopularity, and the public can only pass verdict upon what it has read. The connection seems clear and the proposition proved that the retail bookseller is an almost paramount influence in American literature.

It is interesting to see what follows from this and to note how the retailer in the end can effectually throttle the sham novelist who has fooled the public once. Were it not for the retailer, the sham novelist would get an indefinite number of chances for his life; but so long as the small book-dealer lives and acts, just so long will bad work—and one means by this wholly bad, admittedly bad, hopelessly bad work—fail to trick the reading public twice. Observe now the working of it. Let us take a typical case. A story by an unknown writer is published. By strenuous exploitation the publishers start a vogue. The book begins to sell. The retailer, observing the campaign of publicity managed by the publishers, stocks up with the volume; surely when the publishers are backing the thing so strong it will be a safe venture; surely the demand will be great. It does prove a safe venture; the demand is great; the retailer disposes of fifty, then of a second order of one hundred, then of two hundred, then of five hundred. The book is now in the hands of the public. It is read and found sadly, sadly wanting. It is not a good story; it is trivial; it is insincere. Far and wide the story is condemned.

Meanwhile the unknown writer, now become famous, is writing a second novel. It is finished, issued, and the salesman who travels for the publishers begins to place his orders. The retailer, remembering the success of this author's past venture, readily places a large order. Two hundred is not, in his opinion, an overstock. So it goes all over the country. Returns are made to the author, and he sees that some fifty thousand have been sold. Encouraging, is it not? Yes, fifty thousand have been sold— by the publisher to the retailer; but here is the point—not by the retailer to the public. Of the two hundred our dealer took from the publisher's traveling salesman, one hundred and ninety yet remain upon his counters. The public, fooled once, on the first over-praised, over-exploited book, refuse to be taken in a second time. Who is the loser now? Not the author, who draws royalties on copies sold to the tradesman—the retailer; not the publisher, who makes his profit out of the same transaction; but the retailer, who is loaded down with an unsalable article.

Meanwhile our author writes his third novel. So far as he can see, his second book is as great a popular success as his first. His semiannual statements are there to show it—there it is in black and white; figures can't lie. The third novel is finished and launched. At the end of the first six months after publication day the author gets his publisher's statement of sales. Instead of the expected 10,000 copies sold, behold the figure is a bare 1,500. At the end of the second six months the statement shows about 250. The book has failed. Why? Because the retailer refuses to order it. He has said to the soliciting salesman, "Why should I, in Heaven's name, take a third book by this man when I have yet one hundred and ninety copies of his second novel yet to sell?"

It is hard for the salesman to controvert that argument. He may argue that the third book is a masterpiece, and—mark this—it may in fact be a veritable, actual masterpiece, a wonderful contribution to the world's literature; it is all of no effect. There stands the block of unsold books, 190 strong, and all the eloquence in the world will not argue them

off the counter. After this our author's publisher will have none of his books. Even if he
writes a fourth and submits it, the publisher
incontinently declines it. This author is no
longer a "business proposition."

There cannot but be an element of satisfaction in all this, and a source of comfort to those
who take the welfare of their country's literature seriously to heart. The sham novelist
who is in literature (what shall we say) "for his
own pocket every time" sooner or later meets
the wave of reaction that he cannot stem nor
turn and under which he and his sham are conclusively, definitely and irrevocably buried.
Observe how it works out all down the line.
He fools himself all of the time, he fools the
publisher three times, he fools the retail dealer
twice, and he fools the Great American Public
just exactly once.

AN AMERICAN SCHOOL OF FICTION?

AN AMERICAN SCHOOL OF FICTION?

IT seems to me that it is a proposition not difficult of demonstration that the United States of America has never been able to boast of a school of fiction distinctively its own. And this is all the more singular when one considers that in all other activities Americans are peculiarly independent in thought and in deed, and have acquired abroad a reputation—even a notoriety—for being original.

In the mechanical arts, in the industries, in politics, in business methods, in diplomacy, in ship-building, in war, even in dentistry, if you please—even in the matter of riding race-horses —Americans have evolved their own methods, quite different from European methods.

Hardy and adventurous enough upon all other lines, disdainful of conventions, contemptuous of ancient custom, we yet lag behind in the arts—slow to venture from the path blazed long ago by Old World masters.

It is preëminently so in the fine arts. No sooner does an American resolve upon a career of painting, sculpture or architecture than straight he departs for Paris, the Beaux Arts and the Julien atelier; and, his education finished, returns to propagate French ideas; French methods; and our best paintings to-day are more French than American; French in conception, in composition, in technique and treatment.

I suppose that the nearest we ever came to an organized school of native-born Americans, writing about American things from an American point of view, was in the days of Lowell, Longfellow, Holmes, Whittier and the rest of that illustrious company. But observe: How is this group spoken of and known to literature? Not as the American school, but as the New England school. Even the appellation "New" England as differentiated from "old" England is significant. And New England is not America.

Hawthorne, it will be urged, is a great name among American writers of fiction. Not peculiarly American, however. Not so distinctively and unequivocally as to lay claim to a vigorous original Americanism. "The Scarlet Letter" is not an American story, but rather a story of an English colony on North American soil. "The Marble Faun" is frankly and unreservedly foreign. Even the other novels were pictures of a very limited and circumscribed life—the life of New England again.

Cooper, you will say, was certainly American in attitude and choice of subject; none more so. None less, none less American. As a novelist he is saturated with the romance of the contemporary English story-tellers. It is true that his background is American. But his heroes and heroines talk like the characters out of Bulwer in their most vehement moods, while his Indians stalk through all the melodramatic tableaux of Byron, and declaim in the periods of the border noblemen in the pages of Walter Scott.

Poe we may leave out of classification; he shone in every branch of literature but that of novel-writing. Bret Harte was a writer of short stories and—oh, the pity of it, the folly of it!—abandoned the field with hardly more than a mere surface-scratching.

There can be no doubt that had Mr. Henry James remained in America he would have been our very best writer. If he has been able to seize the character and characteristics so forcibly of a people like the English, foreign to him, different, unfamiliar, what might he not have done in the very midst of his own countrymen, into whose company he was born, reared and educated. All the finish of style, the

marvelous felicity of expression would still have
been his and at the same time, by the very
nature of the life he lived and wrote about,
the concrete, the vigorous, the simple direct
action would have become a part of his work,
instead of the present ultimate vagueness and
indecision that so mars and retards it.

Of all the larger names remain only those
of Mr. Howells and Mr. Clemens. But as the
novelists, as such, are under consideration,
even Mark Twain may be left out of the discussion. American to the core, posterity will
yet know him not as a novel-writer, but as a
humourist. Mr. Howells alone is left, then,
after the elimination is complete. Of all producers of American fiction he has had the broad-
est vision, at once a New Englander and a New
Yorker, an Easterner and—in the Eastern sense
—a Westerner. But one swallow does not make
a summer, nor does one writer constitute a
"school." Mr. Howells has had no successors.
Instead, just as we had with "Lapham"
and "The Modern Instance" laid the foundation of fine, hardy literature, that promised to
be our very, very own, we commence to build
upon it a whole confused congeries of borrowed,
faked, pilfered romanticisms, building a crumbling gothic into a masonry of honest brownstone, or foisting colonial porticos upon façades

of Montpelier granite, and I cannot allow this occasion to pass without protest against what I am sure every serious-minded reader must consider a lamentable discrowning.

Of the latter-day fiction writers Miss Wilkins had more than all others convinced her public of her sincerity. Her field was her own; the place was ceded to her. No other novelist could invade her domain and escape the censure that attaches to imitation. Her public was loyal to her because it believed in her, and it was a foregone conclusion that she would be loyal to it.

More than this: A writer who occupies so eminent a place as Miss Wilkins, who has become so important, who has exerted and still can exert so strong an influence, cannot escape the responsibilities of her position. She cannot belong wholly to herself, cannot be wholly independent. She owes a duty to the literature of her native country.

Yet in spite of all this, and in spite of the fact that those who believe in the future of our nation's letters look to such established reputations as hers to keep the faith, to protest, though it is only by their attitude, silently and with dignity, against corruptions, degradations; in spite of all this, and in the heyday of her power, Miss Wilkins chooses to succumb to the momentary, transitory set of the tide, and forsaking her own particular work, puts forth, one of a hundred others, a "colonial romance." It is a discrowning. It can be considered as no less. A deliberate capitulation to the clamour of the multitude. Possibly the novelist was sincere, but it is perilously improbable that she would have written her "Colonial Romance" had not "colonial romances" been the fashion. On the face of it Miss Wilkins has laid herself open to a suspicion of disingenuousness that every honest critic can only deplore. Even with all the sincerity in the world she had not the right to imperil the faith of her public, to undermine its confidence in her. She was one of the leaders. It is as if a captain, during action, had deserted to the enemy.

It could not have been even for the baser consideration of money. With her success assured in advance Miss Wilkins can be above such influences. Nor of fame. Surely no great distinction centres upon writers of "colonial romances" of late. Only the author herself may know her motives, but we who looked to her to keep the standard firm—and high—have now to regret the misfortune of a leader lost, a cause weakened

However, it is a question after all if a "school,"

understood in the European sense of the word, is possible for America just yet. France has had its schools of naturalism and romance, Russia its schools of realism, England its schools of psychologists. But France, Russia and England now, after so many centuries of growth, may be considered as units. Certain tendencies influence each one over its whole geographical extent at the same time. Its peoples have been welded together to a certain homogeneousness. It is under such conditions that "schools" of fiction, of philosophy, of science and the like arise.

But the United States are not yet, in the European sense, united. We have existed as a nation hardly more than a generation and during that time our peoples have increased largely by emigration. From all over the globe different races have been pouring in upon us. The North has been settled under one system, the South under another, the Middle West under another, the East under another. South Central and Far West under still others. There is no homogeneousness among us as yet. The Westerner thinks along different lines from the Easterner and arrives at different conclusions. What is true of California is false of New York. Mr. Cable's picture of life is a far different thing than that of Mr. Howells.

The "school" implies a rallying of many elements under one standard. But no such thing is possible to-day for American writers. Mr. Hamlin Garland could not merge his personality nor pool his ideals with Edith Wharton. Their conceptions of art are as different as the conditions of life they study in their books.

The school of fiction American in thought, in purpose and in treatment will come in time, inevitably. Meanwhile the best we can expect of the leaders is to remain steadfast, to keep unequivocably to the metes and bounds of the vineyards of their labours; no trespassing, no borrowing, no filching of the grapes of another man's vines. The cultivation of one's own vine is quite sufficient for all energy. We want these vines to grow—in time—to take root deep in American soil so that by and by the fruit shall be all of our own growing.

We do not want—distinctly and vehemently we do not want the vine-grower to leave his own grapes to rot while he flies off to the gathering of—what? The sodden lees of an ancient crushing.

NOVELISTS OF THE FUTURE

NOVELISTS OF THE FUTURE

IT seems to me that a great deal could be said on this subject—a great deal that has not been said before. There are so many novelists these latter days. So many whose works show that they have had no training, and it does seem that so long as the fiction writers of the United States go fumbling and stumbling along in this undisciplined fashion, governed by no rule, observing no formula, setting for themselves no equation to solve, that just so long shall we be far from the desirable thing—an American school of fiction. Just now (let us say that it is a pity) we have no school at all. We acknowledge no master, and we are playing at truant, incorrigible, unmanageable, sailing paper boats in the creek behind the schoolhouse, or fishing with bent pins in the pools and shallows of popular favour. That some catch goldfish there is no great matter, and is no excuse for the truancy. We are not there for the goldfish, if you please, but to remain in the school at work till we have been summoned to stand up in our places and tell the master what we have learned.

There's where we should be, and if we do not observe the rules and conform to some degree of order, we should be rapped on the knuckles or soundly clumped on the head, and by vigorous discipline taught to know that formulas (a—b; a+b) are important things for us to observe, and that each and all of us should address ourselves with all diligence to finding the value of x in our problems.

It is the class in the Production of Original Fiction which of all the school contains the most truants. Indeed, its members believe that schooling for them is unnecessary. Not so with the other classes. Not one single member of any single one of them who does not believe that he must study first if he would produce afterward. Observe, there on the lower benches, the assiduous little would-be carpenters and stone-masons; how carefully they con their tables of measurement, their squares and compasses. "Ah, the toilers," you say, "the grubby manual fellows—of course they must learn their trade!"

Very well, then. Consider—higher up the class, on the very front row of benches—the Fine Arts row, the little painters and architects and musicians and actors of the future. See how painfully they study, and study and study. The little stone-mason will graduate in a few months; but for these others of the Fine Arts classes there is no such thing as graduation. For them there shall never be a diploma, signed and sealed, giving them the right to call themselves perfected at their work. All their lives they shall be students. In the vacations —maybe—they write, or build, or sing, or act, but soon again they are back to the benches, studying, studying always; working as never carpenter or stone-mason worked. Now and then they get a little medal, a bit of gold and enamel, a bow of ribbon, that is all; the stone-mason would disdain it, would seek it for the value of the metal in it. The Fine Arts people treasure it as the veteran treasures his cross.

And these little medals you—the truants, the bad boys of the paper boats and the goldfish— you want them, too; you claim them and clamour for them. You who declare that no study is necessary for you; you who are not content with your catch of goldfish, you must have the bits of ribbon and enamel, too. Have you deserved them? Have you worked for them? Have you found the value of x in your equation? Have you solved the parenthesis of your problem? Have you even done the problem at all? Have you even glanced or guessed at the equation? The shame of it be upon you! Come in from the goldfish and go to work, or stay altogether at the fishing and admit that you are not deserving of the medal which the master gives as a reward of merit.

"But there are no books that we can study," you contest. "The architect and the musician, the painter and the actor—all of these have books ready to hand; they can learn from codified, systematized knowledge. For the novelist, where is there of cut-and-dried science that he can learn that will help him?"

And that is a good contention. No, there are no such books. Of all the arts, the art of fiction has no handbook. By no man's teaching can we learn the knack of putting a novel together in the best way. No one has ever risen to say, "Here is how the plan should be; thus and so should run the outline."

We admit the fact, but neither does that excuse the goldfishing and the paper-boat business. Some day the handbook may be compiled—it is quite possible—but meanwhile, and *faute de mieux*, there is that which you may study better than all handbooks.

Observe, now. Observe, for instance, the little painter scholars. On the fly-leaves of their schoolbooks they are making pictures— of what? Remember it, remember it and remember it—of the people around them. So is the actor, so the musician—all of the occu-

pants of the Fine Arts bench. They are studying one another quite as much as their books
—even more, and they will tell you that it is
the most important course in the curriculum.

You—the truant little would-be novelist—
you can do this, quite as easily as they, and for
you it is all the more important, for you must
make up for the intimate knowledge of your
fellows what you are forced to lack in the igno-
rance of forms. But you cannot get this
knowledge out there behind the schoolhouse—
hooking goldfish. Come in at the tap of the
bell and, though you have no books, make
pictures on your slate, pictures of the Fine
Arts bench struggling all their lives for the
foolish little medals, pictures of the grubby
little boys in the stone-mason's corner, jeering
the art classes for their empty toiling. The
more you make these pictures, the better you
shall do them. That is the kind of studying
you can do, and from the study of your fellows
you shall learn more than from the study of all
the text-books that ever will be written.

But to do this you must learn to sit very
quiet, and be very watchful, and so train your
eyes and ears that every sound and every
sight shall be significant to you and shall
supply all the deficiency made by the absence
of text-books.

This, then, to drop a very protracted allegory, seems to be the proper training of the novelist: The achieving less of an aggressive faculty of research than of an attitude of mind —a receptivity, an acute sensitiveness. And this can be acquired.

But it cannot be acquired by shutting oneself in one's closet, by a withdrawal from the world, and that, so it would appear, is just the mistake so many would-be fiction writers allow themselves. They would make the art of the novelist an aristocracy, a thing exclusive, to be guarded from contact with the vulgar, humdrum, bread-and-butter business of life, to be kept unspotted from the world, considering it the result of inspirations, of exaltations, of subtleties and—above all things—of refinement, a sort of velvet jacket affair, a studio hocus-pocus, a thing loved of women and of esthetes.

What a folly! Of all the arts it is the most virile; of all the arts it will not, will not, will not flourish indoors. Dependent solely upon fidelity to life for existence, it must be practised in the very heart's heart of life, on the street corner, in the market-place, not in the studios. God enlighten us! It is not an affair of women and esthetes, and the muse of American fiction is no chaste, delicate, superfine mademoi-

selle of delicate poses and "elegant" attitudin-
izings, but a robust, red-armed *bonne femme*,
who rough-shoulders her way among men and
among affairs, who finds a healthy pleasure in
the jostlings of the mob and a hearty delight
in the honest, rough-and-tumble, Anglo-Saxon
give-and-take knockabout that for us means
life. Choose her, instead of the sallow, pale-
faced statue-creature, with the foolish tablets
and foolish, upturned eyes, and she will lead
you as brave a march as ever drum tapped to.
Stay at her elbow and obey her as she tells you
to open your eyes and ears and heart, and as you
go she will show things wonderful beyond
wonder in this great, new, blessed country of
ours, will show you a life untouched, untried,
full of new blood and promise and vigour.

She is a Child of the People, this muse of our
fiction of the future, and the wind of a new
country, a new heaven and a new earth is in
her face and has blown her hair from out the
fillets that the Old World muse has bound across
her brow, so that it is all in disarray. The tan
of the sun is on her cheeks, and the dust of the
highway is thick upon her buskin, and the
elbowing of many men has torn the robe of her,
and her hands are hard with the grip of many
things. She is hail-fellow-well-met with every
one she meets, unashamed to know the clown

and unashamed to face the king, a hardy, vigorous girl, with an arm as strong as a man's and a heart as sensitive as a child's.

Believe me, she will lead you far from the studios and the esthetes, the velvet jackets and the uncut hair, far from the sexless creatures who cultivate their little art of writing as the fancier cultivates his orchid. Tramping along, then, with a stride that will tax your best paces, she will lead you—if you are humble with her and honest with her—straight into a World of Working Men, crude of speech, swift of action, strong of passion, straight to the heart of a new life, on the borders of a new time, and there and there only will you learn to know the stuff of which must come the American fiction of the future.

A PLEA FOR ROMANTIC FICTION

A PLEA FOR ROMANTIC FICTION

LET us at the start make a distinction. Observe that one speaks of romanticism and not sentimentalism. One claims that the latter is as distinct from the former as is that other form of art which is called Realism. Romance has been often put upon and overburdened by being forced to bear the onus of abuse that by right should fall to sentiment; but the two should be kept very distinct, for a very high and illustrious place will be claimed for romance, while sentiment will be handed down the scullery stairs.

Many people to-day are composing mere sentimentalism, and calling it and causing it to be called romance; so with those who are too busy to think much upon these subjects, but who none the less love honest literature, Romance, too, has fallen into disrepute. Consider now the cut-and-thrust stories. They are all labeled Romances, and it is very easy to get the impression that Romance must be an affair of cloaks and daggers, or moonlight and golden hair. But this is not so at all. The true Romance is a more serious business than this. It is not merely a conjurer's trick-box, full of flimsy quackeries, tinsel and claptraps, meant only to amuse, and relying upon deception to do even that. Is it not something better than this? Can we not see in it an instrument, keen, finely tempered, flawless—an instrument with which we may go straight through the clothes and tissues and wrappings of flesh down deep into the red, living heart of things?

Is all this too subtle, too merely speculative and intrinsic, too *precieuse* and nice and "literary"? Devoutly one hopes the contrary. So much is made of so-called Romanticism in present-day fiction that the subject seems worthy of discussion, and a protest against the misuse of a really noble and honest formula of literature appeals to be timely—misuse, that is, in the sense of limited use. Let us suppose for the moment that a romance can be made out of a cut-and-thrust business. Good Heavens, are there no other things that are romantic, even in this—falsely, falsely called —humdrum world of to-day? Why should it be that so soon as the novelist addresses himself —seriously—to the consideration of contemporary life he must abandon Romance and take up that harsh, loveless, colourless, blunt tool called Realism?

Now, let us understand at once what is meant by Romance and what by Realism. Romance, I take it, is the kind of fiction that takes cognizance of variations from the type of normal life. Realism is the kind of fiction that confines itself to the type of normal life. According to this definition, then, Romance may even treat of the sordid, the unlovely—as for instance, the novels of M. Zola. (Zola has been dubbed a Realist, but he is, on the contrary, the very head of the Romanticists.) Also, Realism, used as it sometimes is as a term of reproach, need not be in the remotest sense or degree offensive, but on the other hand respectable as a church and proper as a deacon —as, for instance, the novels of Mr. Howells.

The reason why one claims so much for Romance, and quarrels so pointedly with Realism, is that Realism stultifies itself. It notes only the surface of things. For it, Beauty is not even skin deep, but only a geometrical plane, without dimensions and depth, a mere outside. Realism is very excellent so far as it goes, but it goes no further than the Realist himself can actually see, or actually hear. Realism is minute; it is the drama of a broken teacup, the tragedy of a walk down the block, the excitement of an afternoon call, the adventure of an invitation to dinner. It is the visit to my neighbour's house, a formal visit, from which I may draw no conclusions. I see my neighbour and his friends—very, oh, such very! probable people—and that is all. Realism bows upon the doormat and goes away and says to me, as we link arms on the sidewalk: "That is life." And I say it is not. It is not, as you would very well see if you took Romance with you to call upon your neighbour.

Lately you have been taking Romance a weary journey across the water—ages and the flood of years—and haling her into the fusby, musty, worm-eaten, moth-riddled, rust-corroded "Grandes Salles" of the Middle Ages and the Renaissance, and she has found the drama of a bygone age for you there. But would you take her across the street to your neighbour's front parlour (with the bisque fisher-boy on the mantel and the photograph of Niagara Falls on glass hanging in the front window); would you introduce her there? Not you. Would you take a walk with her on Fifth Avenue, or Beacon Street, or Michigan Avenue? No, indeed. Would you choose her for a companion of a morning spent in Wall Street, or an afternoon in the Waldorf-Astoria? You just guess you would not.

She would be out of place, you say—inappropriate. She might be awkward in my neighbour's front parlour, and knock over the little bisque fisher-boy. Well, she might. If she did, you might find underneath the base of the statuette, hidden away, tucked away— what? God knows. But something that would be a complete revelation of my neighbour's secretest life.

So you think Romance would stop in the front parlour and discuss medicated flannels and mineral waters with the ladies? Not for more than five minutes. She would be off up-stairs with you, prying, peeping, peering into the closets of the bedroom, into the nursery, into the sitting-room; yes, and into that little iron box screwed to the lower shelf of the closet in the library; and into those compartments and pigeon-holes of the *secretaire* in the study. She would find a heartache (maybe) between the pillows of the mistress's bed, and a memory carefully secreted in the master's deed-box. She would come upon a great hope amid the books and papers of the study-table of the young man's room, and—perhaps— who knows—an affair, or, great Heavens, an intrigue, in the scented ribbons and gloves and hairpins of the young lady's bureau. And she would pick here a little and there a little, making up a bag of hopes and fears and a pack-age of joys and sorrows—great ones, mind you

—and then come down to the front door, and, stepping out into the street, hand you the bags and package and say to you—"That is Life!"

Romance does very well in the castles of the Middle Ages and the Renaissance chateaux, and she has the *entree* there and is very well received.   That is all well and good.   But let us protest against limiting her to such places and such times.   You will find her, I grant you, in the chatelaine's chamber and the dungeon of the man-at-arms; but, if you choose to look for her, you will find her equally at home in the brownstone house on the corner and in the office-building downtown.   And this very day, in this very hour, she is sitting among the rags and wretchedness, the dirt and despair of the tenements of the East Side of New York.

"What?" I hear you say, "look for Romance —the lady of the silken robes and golden crown, our beautiful, chaste maiden of soft voice and gentle eyes—look for her among the vicious ruffians, male and female, of Allen Street and Mulberry Bend?"   I tell you she is there, and to your shame be it said you will not know her in those surroundings.   You, the aristocrats, who demand the fine linen and the purple in your fiction; you, the sensitive, the delicate, who will associate with your Romance only so long as she wears a silken gown.   You will not

follow her to the slums, for you believe that
Romance should only amuse and entertain you,
singing you sweet songs and touching the harp
of silver strings with rosy-tipped fingers. If
haply she should call to you from the squalour
of a dive, or the awful degradation of a dis-
orderly house, crying: "Look! listen! This,
too, is life. These, too, are my children! Look
at them, know them and, knowing, help!"
Should she call thus you would stop your ears;
you would avert your eyes and you would
answer, "Come from there, Romance. Your
place is not there!" And you would make of
her a harlequin, a tumbler, a sword-dancer,
when, as a matter of fact, she should be by
right divine a teacher sent from God.

She will not often wear the robe of silk, the
gold crown, the jeweled shoon; will not always
sweep the silver harp. An iron note is hers
if so she choose, and coarse garments, and
stained hands; and, meeting her thus, it is for
you to know her as she passes—know her for
the same young queen of the blue mantle
and lilies. She can teach you if you will be
humble to learn—teach you by showing.
God help you if at last you take from Romance
her mission of teaching; if you do not believe
that she has a purpose—a nobler purpose and a
mightier than mere amusement, mere enter-

tainment. Let Realism do the entertaining
with its meticulous presentation of teacups,
rag carpets, wall-paper and haircloth sofas,
stopping with these, going no deeper than it
sees, choosing the ordinary, the untroubled,
the commonplace.

But to Romance belongs the wide world for
range, and the unplumbed depths of the human
heart, and the mystery of sex, and the problems
of life, and the black, unsearched penetralia
of the soul of man. You, the indolent, must
not always be amused. What matter the
silken clothes, what matter the prince's houses?
Romance, too, is a teacher, and if—throwing
aside the purple—she wears the camel's-hair
and feeds upon the locusts, it is to cry aloud
unto the people, "Prepare ye the way of the
Lord; make straight his path."

A PROBLEM IN FICTION

A PROBLEM IN FICTION

SO many people—writers more especially —claim stridently and with a deal of gesturing that because a thing has happened it is therefore true. They have written a story, let us say, and they bring it to you to criticize. You lay your finger upon a certain passage and say "Not true to life." The author turns on you and then annihilates you —in his own mind—with the words, "But it actually happened." Of course, then, it must be true. On the contrary, it is accurate only.

For the assumption is, that truth is a higher power of accuracy—that the true thing includes the accurate; and assuming this, the authors of novels—that are not successful—suppose that if they are accurate, if they tell the thing just as they saw it, that they are truthful. It is not difficult to show that a man may be as accurate as the spectroscope and yet lie like a Chinese diplomat. As for instance: Let us suppose you have never seen a sheep, never heard of sheep, don't know sheep from shavings. It devolves upon me to enlighten your ıgnorance. I go out into the field and select from the flock a black sheep, bring it before you, and, with the animal there under our eyes, describe it in detail, faithfully, omitting nothing, falsifying nothing, exaggerating nothing. I am painfully accurate. But you go away with the untrue conviction that all sheep are black! I have been accurate, but I have not been true.

So it is with very, very many novels, written with all earnestness and seriousness. Every incident has happened in real life, and because it is picturesque, because it is romantic, because, in a word, it is like some other novel, it is seized upon at once, and serves as the nucleus of a tale. Then, because this tale fails of success, because it fails to impress, the author blames the public, not himself. He thinks he has gone to life for his material, and so must be original, new and true. It is not so. Life itself is not always true; strange as it may seem, you may be able to say that life is not always true to life—from the point of view of the artist. It happened once that it was my unfortunate duty to tell a certain man of the violent death of his only brother, whom he had left well and happy but an hour before. This is how he took it: He threw up both hands and staggered back, precisely as they do in melodrama, exclaiming all in a breath: "Oh, my God! This is terrible! What will mother say?" You may say what you please, this man was not true to life. From the point of view of the teller of tales he was theatrical, false, untrue, and though the incident was an actual fact and though the emotion was real, it had no value as "material," and no fiction writer in his senses would have thought of using it in his story.

Naturally enough it will be asked what, then, is the standard. How shall the writer guide himself in the treatment of a pivotal, critical scene, or how shall the reader judge whether or not he is true. Perhaps, after all, the word "seem," and not the word "true," is the most important. Of course no good novelist, no good artist, can represent life as it actually is. Nobody can, for nobody knows. Who is to say what life actually is? It seems easy—easy for us who have it and live in it and see it and hear it and feel it every millionth part of every second of the time. I say that life is actually this or that, and you say it is something else, and number three says "Lo! here," and number four says "Lo! there." Not even science is going to help you; no two photographs, even, will convey just the same impression of the same actuality; and here we are dealing not with science, but with art, that instantly involves the personality of the artist and all that that means. Even the same artist will not see the same thing twice exactly alike. His personality is one thing to-day and another thing to-morrow—is one thing before dinner and another thing after it. How, then, to determine what life actually is?

The point is just this. In the fine arts we do not care one little bit about what life actually is, but what it looks like to an interesting, impressionable man, and if he tells his story or paints his picture so that the majority of intelligent people will say, "Yes, that must have been just about what would have happened under those circumstances," he is true. His accuracy cuts no figure at all. He need not be accurate if he does not choose to be. If he sees fit to be inaccurate in order to make his point—so only his point be the conveying of a truthful impression—that is his affair. We have nothing to do with that. Consider the study of a French cuirassier by Detaille; where the sunlight strikes the brown coat of the horse, you will see, if you look close, a mere smear of blue—light blue. This is inaccurate. The horse is not blue, nor has he any blue spots. Stand at the proper distance and the blue smear resolves itself into the glossy reflection of the sun, and the effect is true,

And in fiction: Take the fine scene in "Ivanhoe," where Rebecca, looking from the window, describes the assault upon the outer walls of the castle to the wounded knight lying on the floor in the room behind her. If you stop and think, you will see that Rebecca never could have found such elaborate language under the stress of so great excitement—those cleverly managed little climaxes in each phrase, building up to the great climax of the paragraph, all the play of rhetoric, all the nice chain and adjustment of adjectives; she could not possibly have done it. Neither you nor I, nor any of us, with all the thought and time and labour at our command, could have ever written the passage. But is it not admirably true— true as the truth itself? It is not accurate: it is grossly, ludicrously inaccurate; but the fire and leap and vigour of it; there is where the truth is. Scott wanted you to get an impression of that assault on the barbican, and you do get it. You can hear those axes on the outer gate as plainly as Rebecca could; you can see the ladders go up, can hear them splinter, can see and feel and know all the rush and trample and smashing of that fine fight, with the Fetter-lock Knight always to the fore, as no merely accurate description—accurate to five points of decimals—could ever present it.

So that one must remember the distinction, and claim no more for accuracy than it deserves —and that's but little. Anybody can be accurate—the man with the foot-rule is that. Accuracy is the attainment of small minds, the achievement of the commonplace, a mere machine-made thing that comes with niggardly research and ciphering and mensuration and the multiplication table, good in its place, so only the place is very small. In fiction it can under certain circumstances be dispensed with altogether. It is not a thing to be striven for. To be true is the all-important business, and, once attaining that, "all other things shall be added unto you." Paint the horse peagreen if it suits your purpose; fill the mouth of Rebecca with gasconades and rhodomontades interminable: these things do not matter. It is truth that matters, and the point is whether the daubs of pea-green will look like horseflesh and the mouth-filling words create the impression of actual battle.

WHY WOMEN SHOULD WRITE
THE BEST NOVELS

WHY WOMEN SHOULD WRITE THE BEST NOVELS

IT is rather curious upon reflection and upon looking over the rank and file of achievement during the period of recorded history, to observe that of all the occupations at first exclusively followed by men, that of writing has been—in all civilizations and among all people—one of the very first to be successfully —mark the qualification of the adverb—to be successfully invaded by women. We hear of women who write poetry long before we hear of women who paint pictures or perform upon musical instruments or achieve distinction upon the stage.

It would seem as if, of all the arts, that of writing is the one to which women turn the quickest. Great success in the sciences or in mercantile pursuits is, of course, out of the question, so that—as at the first—it may be said, speaking largely, that of all the masculine occupations, that of writing is the first to be adopted by women.

If it is the first it must be because it is the easiest. Now to go very far back to the earliest beginnings, all occupations, whether artistic or otherwise, were the prerogative of the male; considering this fact, I say, does it not follow, or would not the inference be strong, that—given an equal start—women would write more readily than men, would do so because they could do so; that writing is a feminine—not accomplishment merely—but gift.

So that the whole matter leads up to the point one wishes to make, namely, that here, in our present day and time, it should be easier for women to write well than for men. And as writing to-day means the writing of fiction, we arrive, somewhat deviously and perhaps— after jumping many gaps and weak spots en route—a little lamely, at the very last result of all, which is this: Women should be able to write better novels than men.

But under modern conditions there are many more reasons for this success of women in fiction than merely a natural inherent gift of expression.

One great reason is leisure. The average man, who must work for a living, has no time to write novels, much less to get into that frame of mind, or to assume that mental attitude by means of which he is able to see possibilities for fictitious narrative in the life around him. But, as yet, few women (compared with the armies of male workers) have to work for a living, and it is an unusual state of affairs in which the average woman of moderate circumstances could not, if she would, take from three to four hours a day from her household duties to devote to any occupation she deemed desirable.

Another reason is found, one believes, in the nature of women's education. From almost the very first the young man studies with an eye to business or to a profession. In many State colleges nowadays all literary courses, except the most elementary—which, indeed, have no place in collegiate curriculums—are optional. But what girls' seminary does not prescribe the study of literature through all its three or four years, making of this study a matter of all importance? And while the courses of literature do not, by any manner of means, make a novelist, they familiarize the student with style and the means by which words are put together. The more one reads the easier one writes.

Then, too (though this reason lies not so much in modern conditions as in basic principles), there is the matter of temperament. The average man is a rectangular, square-cut, matter-of-fact, sober-minded animal who does not receive impressions easily, who is not troubled with emotions and has no over-mastering desire to communicate his sensations to anybody. But the average woman is just the reverse of all these. She is impressionable, emotional and communicative. And impressionableness, emotionality and communicativeness are three very important qualities of mind that make for novel writing.

The modern woman, then, in a greater degree than her contemporaneous male, has the leisure for novel writing, has the education and has the temperament. She should be able to write better novels, and as a matter of fact she does not. It is, of course, a conceded fact that there have been more great men novelists than women novelists, and that to-day the producers of the best fiction are men and not women. There are probably more women trying to write novels than there are men, but for all this it must be admitted that the ranks of the "arrived" are recruited from the razor contingent.

Why, then, with such a long start and with so many advantages of temperament, opportunity and training should it be that women do not write better novels than men?

One believes that the answer is found in the fact that life is more important than literature, and in the wise, wise, old, old adage that experience is the best teacher. Of all the difficult things that enter into the learning of a most difficult profession, the most difficult of all for the intended novelist to acquire is the fact that life is better than literature. The amateur will say this with conviction, will preach it in public and practise the exact reverse in private. But it still remains true that all the temperament, all the sensitiveness to impressions, all the education in the world will not help one little, little bit in the writing of the novel if life itself, the crude, the raw, the vulgar, if you will, is not studied. An hour's experience is worth ten years of study—of reading other people's books. But this fact is ignored, and the future writer of what it is hoped will be the great novel of his day and age studies the thoughts and products of some other writer, of some other great novel, of some other day and age, in the hope that thereby much may be learned. And much will be learned —very much, indeed—of the methods of construction; and if the tyro only has wits enough to study the great man's formula, well and good. But the fascination of a great story-writer— especially upon the young, untried little story-writer—is strong, and before the latter is well aware he is taking from the big man that which

he has no right to take.　He is taking his code
of ethics, his view of life, his personality, even
to the very incidents and episodes of his story.
He is studying literature and not life.

If he had gone direct to life itself, all would
have been different.　He would have developed
in his own code, his own personality, and he
would have found incidents and episodes that
were new—yes, and strikingly forceful, better
than any he could have imagined or stolen,
and which were all his own.　In the end, if the
gods gave him long life and a faculty of appli-
cation, he would have evolved into something
of a writer of fiction.

All this digression is to try to state the
importance of actual life and actual experience,
and it bears upon the subject in hand in this,
that women who have all the other qualifications of good novelists are, because of nature
and character that invariably goes with these
qualifications, shut away from the study of,
and the association with, the most important
thing of all for them—real life.　Even making
allowances for the emancipation of the New
Woman, the majority of women still lead, in
comparison with men, secluded lives.　The
woman who is impressionable is by reason
of this very thing sensitive (indeed, sensitiveness and impressionableness mean almost

the same thing), and it is inconceivably hard for the sensitive woman to force herself into the midst of that great, grim complication of men's doings that we call life. And even admitting that she finds in herself the courage to do this, she lacks the knowledge to use knowledge thus gained. The faculty of selection comes even to men only after many years of experience.

So much for causes exterior to herself, and it is well to admit at once that the exterior causes are by far the most potent and the most important; but there are perhaps causes to be found in the make-up of the woman herself which keep her from success in fiction. Is it not a fact that protracted labour of the mind tells upon a woman quicker than upon a man. Be it understood that no disparagement, no invidious comparison is intended. Indeed, it is quite possible that her speedier mental fatigue is due to the fact that the woman possesses the more highly specialized organ.

A man may grind on steadily for an almost indefinite period, when a woman at the same task would begin, after a certain point, to "feel her nerves," to chafe, to fret, to try to do too much, to polish too highly, to develop more perfectly. Then come fatigue, harassing doubts, more nerves, a touch of hysteria occasionally, exhaustion, and in the end complete discouragement and a final abandonment of the enterprise: and who shall say how many good, even great, novels have remained half written, to be burned in the end, because their women authors mistook lack of physical strength for lack of genuine ability?

SIMPLICITY IN ART

SIMPLICITY IN ART

ONCE upon a time I had occasion to buy so uninteresting a thing as a silver soup-ladle. The salesman at the silversmith's was obliging and for my inspection brought forth quite an array of ladles. But my purse was flaccid, anemic, and I must pick and choose with all the discrimination in the world. I wanted to make a brave showing with my gift—to get a great deal for my money. I went through a world of soup-ladles—ladles with gilded bowls, with embossed handles, with chased arabesques, but there were none to my taste. "Or perhaps," says the salesman, "you would care to look at something like this," and he brought out a ladle that was as plain and as unadorned as the unclouded sky— and about as beautiful. Of all the others this was the most to my liking. But the price! ah, that anemic purse; and I must put it from me! It was nearly double the cost of any of the rest. And when I asked why, the salesman said:

"You see, in this highly ornamental ware the flaws of the material don't show, and you can cover up a blow-hole or the like by wreaths and beading. But this plain ware has got to be the very best. Every defect is apparent."

And there, if you please, is a conclusive comment upon the whole business—a final basis of comparison of all things, whether commercial or artistic; the bare dignity of the unadorned that may stand before the world all unashamed, panoplied rather than clothed in the consciousness of perfection. We of this latter day, we painters and poets and writers—artists—must labour with all the wits of us, all the strength of us, and with all that we have of ingenuity and perseverance to attain simplicity. But it has not always been so. At the very earliest, men—forgotten, ordinary men—were born with an easy, unblurred vision that to-day we would hail as marvelous genius. Suppose, for instance, the New Testament was all unwritten and one of us were called upon to tell the world that Christ was born, to tell of how we had seen Him, that this was the Messiah. How the adjectives would marshal upon the page, how the exclamatory phrases would cry out, how we would elaborate and elaborate, and how our rhetoric would flare and blazen till—so we should imagine—the ear would ring and the very eye would be dazzled; and even then we would believe that our words were all so few and feeble. It is beyond words, we should vociferate. So it would be. That is very true—words of ours. Can you not see how we should dramatize it? We would make a point of the transcendent stillness of the hour, of the deep blue of the Judean midnight, of the lip-lapping of Galilee, the murmur of Jordan, the peacefulness of sleeping Jerusalem. Then the stars, the descent of the angel, the shepherds— all the accessories. And our narrative would be as commensurate with the subject as the flippant smartness of a "bright" reporter in the Sistine chapel. We would be striving to cover up our innate incompetence, our impotence to do justice to the mighty theme by elaborateness of design and arabesque intricacy of rhetoric.

But on the other hand—listen:

"The days were accomplished that she should be delivered, and she brought forth her first born son and wrapped him in swaddling clothes and laid him in a manger, because there was no room for them in the inn."

Simplicity could go no further. Absolutely not one word unessential, not a single adjective that is not merely descriptive. The whole matter stated with the terseness of a military report, and yet—there is the epic, the world epic, beautiful, majestic, incomparably dignified, and no ready writer, no Milton nor Shakspere, with all the wealth of their vocabularies, with all the resources of their genius, with all their power of simile or metaphor, their pomp of eloquence or their royal pageantry of hexameters, could produce the effect contained in these two simple declarative sentences.

The mistake that we little people are so prone to make is this: that the more intense the emotional quality of the scene described, the more "vivid," the more exalted, the more richly coloured we suppose should be the language.

When the crisis of the tale is reached there is where we like the author to spread himself, to show the effectiveness of his treatment. But if we would only pause to take a moment's thought we must surely see that the simplest, even the barest statement of fact is only not all-sufficient but all-appropriate.

Elaborate phrase, rhetoric, the intimacy of metaphor and allegory and simile is forgivable for the unimportant episodes where the interest of the narrative is languid; where we are willing to watch the author's ingenuity in the matter of scrolls and fretwork and mosaics-rococo work. But when the catastrophe comes, when the narrative swings clear upon its pivot and we are lifted with it from out the world of our surroundings, we want to forget the author. We want no adjectives to blur our substantives. The substantives may now speak for themselves. We want no metaphor, no simile to make clear the matter. If at this moment of drama and intensity the matter is not of itself preëminently clear no verbiage, however ingenious, will clarify it. Heighten the effect. Does exclamation and heroics on the part of the bystanders ever make the curbstone drama more poignant? Who would care to see Niagara through coloured fire and calcium lights.

The simple treatment, whether of a piece of silversmith work or of a momentous religious epic, is always the most difficult of all. It demands more of the artist. The unskilful story-teller as often as not tells the story to himself as well as to his hearers as he goes along. Not sure of exactly how he is to reach the end, not sure even of the end itself, he must feel his way from incident to incident, from page to page, fumbling, using many words, repeating himself. To hide the confusion there is one resource—elaboration, exaggerated outline, violent colour, till at last the unstable outline disappears under the accumulation, and the reader is to be so dazzled with the wit of the dialogue, the smartness of the repartee, the felicity of the diction, that he will not see the gaps and lapses in the structure itself—just as the "nobby" drummer wears a wide and showy scarf to conceal a soiled shirt-bosom.

But in the master-works of narrative there is none of this shamming, no shoddyism, no humbug.   There is little more than bare outline, but in the care with which it is drawn, how much thought, what infinite pains go to the making of each stroke, so that when it is made it falls just at the right place and exactly in its right sequence.   This attained, what need is there for more?   Comment is superfluous.   If the author make the scene appear terrible to the reader he need not say in himself or in the mouth of some protagonist, "It is terrible!"   If the picture is pathetic so that he who reads must weep, how superfluous, how intrusive should the author exclaim, "It was pitiful to the point of tears."   If beautiful, we do not want him to tell us so.   We want him to make it beautiful and our own appreciation will supply the adjectives.

Beauty, the ultimate philosophical beauty, is not a thing of elaboration, but on the contrary of an almost barren nudity: a jewel may be an exquisite gem, a woman may have a beautiful arm, but the bracelet does not make the arm more beautiful, nor the arm the bracelet. One must admire them separately, and the moment that the jewel ceases to have a value or a reason upon the arm it is better in the case, where it may enjoy an undivided attention.

But after so many hundreds of years of art and artists, of civilization and progress, we have got so far away from the sane old homely uncomplex way of looking out at the world that the simple things no longer charm, and the simple declarative sentence, straightforward, plain, seems flat to our intellectual palate—flat and tasteless and crude.

What we would now call simple our forbears would look upon as a farrago of gimcrackery, and all our art—the art of the better-minded of us—is only a striving to get back to the unblurred, direct simplicity of those writers who could see that the Wonderful, the Counselor, the mighty God, the Prince of Peace, could be laid in a manger and yet be the Saviour of the world.

It is this same spirit, this disdaining of simplicity that has so warped and inflated The First Story, making of it a pomp, an affair of gold-embroidered vestments and costly choirs, of marbles, of jeweled windows and of incense, unable to find the thrill as formerly in the plain and humble stable, and the brown-haired, grave-eyed peasant girl, with her little baby; unable to see the beauty in the crumbling mud walls, the low-ceiled interior, where the only incense was the sweet smell of the cow's breath, the only vestments the swaddling clothes, rough, coarse-fibered, from the hand-looms of Nazareth, the only pomp the scanty gifts of three old men, and the only chanting the crooning of a young mother holding her first-born babe upon her breast.

SALT AND SINCERITY

SALT AND SINCERITY

I

IF the signs of the times may be read aright, and the future forecasted, the volume of short stories is in a fair way of becoming a "rare book." Fewer and fewer of this kind of literature are published every year, and only within the last week one of the foremost of the New York publishers has said that, so far as the material success was concerned, he would prefer to undertake a book of poems rather than a book of stories. Also he explains why. And this is the interesting thing. One has always been puzzled to account for this lapse from a former popularity of a style of fiction certainly legitimate and incontestably entertaining. The publisher in question cites the cheap magazines—the monthlies and weeklies—as the inimical factors. The people go to them for their short stories, not to the cloth-bound volumes for sale at a dollar or a dollar and a half. Why not, if the cheap magazines give "just as good"? Often, too, they give the very same stories which, later, are republished in book form. As the case stands now, any fairly diligent reader of two or three of the more important monthlies and weeklies may anticipate the contents of the entire volume, and very naturally he cannot be expected to pay a dollar for something he already has.

Or even suppose—as is now generally demanded by the publisher—the author adds to the forthcoming collection certain hitherto unpublished stories. Even this does not tempt the buyer. Turning over the leaves at the bookseller's, he sees two, three, five, half a dozen familiar titles. "Come," says he, "I have read three-fourths of this book already. I have no use for it."

It is quite possible that this state of affairs will produce important results. It is yet, perhaps, too soon to say, but it is not outside the range of the probable that, in America at least, it will, in time to come, engender a decay in the quality of the short story. It may be urged that the high prices paid by periodicals to the important short-story writers —the best men—will still act as a stimulus to production. But this does not follow by any means. Authors are queer cattle. They do not always work for money, but sometimes for a permanent place in the eyes of the world. Books give them this—not fugitive short stories, published here and there, and at irregular intervals. Reputations that have been made by short stories published in periodicals may be counted upon the fingers of one hand. The "life of a novel"—to use a trade term—is to a certain extent indeterminable. The life of a short story, be it never so excellent, is prolonged only till the next issue of the periodical in which it has appeared. If the periodical is a weekly it will last a week, if a monthly a month—*and not a day more.* If very good, it will create a demand for another short story by the same author, but that one particular contribution, the original one, is irretrievably and hopelessly dead.

If the author is in literature "for his own pocket every time," he is generally willing to accept the place of a short-story writer. If he is one of the "best men," working for a "permanent place," he will turn his attention and time, his best efforts, to the writing of novels, reverting to the short story only when necessary for the sake of boiling the Pot and chasing the Wolf. He will abandon the field to the inferior men, or enter it only to dispose of "copy" which does not represent him at his best. And, as a result, the quality of the short story will decline more and more.

So, "taking one consideration with another,"

it may be appropriate to inquire if it is not possible that the American short story is liable to decline in quality and standard of excellence.

And now comes again this question addressed to certain authors, "Which book do you consider your best?" and a very industrious and painstaking person is giving the answer to the world.

To what end it is difficult to see. Who cares which of the "Waverleys" Sir Walter thought his best? or which of the Rougon-Maquart M. Zola favours the most? The author's point of view is very different from yours— the reader's. Which one do *you* think the best? That's the point. Do you not see that in the author's opinion the novel he is working on at the moment, or which is in press and about to appear—in fine, the last one written— is for a very long time the best he has done? He would be a very poor kind of novelist if he did not think that.

And even in retrospect his opinion as to "his best book" is not necessarily final. For he will see good points in "unsuccessful" novels that the public and critics have never and will never discover; and also defects in what the world considers his masterpiece that for him spoil the entire story. His best novel is, as was said, the last he has written, or—and this more especially—the one he is *going* to write. For to a certain extent this is true of every author, whether fiction writer or not. *Though he very often does better than he thinks he can, he never does so well as he knows he might.*

His best book is the one that he never quite succeeds in getting hold of firmly enough to commit to paper. It is always just beyond him. Next year he is going to think it out, or the next after that, and instead he compromises on something else, and his *chef d'œuvre* is always a little ahead of him. If this, too, were not so, he would be a poor kind of writer. So that it seems to me the most truthful answer to the question, "What is your best book?' would be, "The one I shall never write."

Another ideal that such of the "people who imagine a vain thing" have long been pursuing is an English Academy of letters, and now that "the British Academy for the promotion of Historical, Philosophical and Philological studies" has been proposed, the old discussion is revived, and especially in England there is talk of a British Academy, something on the same lines as the *Académie Française*, which shall tend to promote and reward particularly the production of good fiction. In a word, it would be a distinction reserved only for the worthy, a charmed circle that would open only to the elite upon the vote of those already admitted. The proposition strikes one as preëminently ridiculous. Literature is of all arts the most democratic; it is of, by and for the people in a fuller measure than even government itself. And one makes the assertion without forgetting that fine mouth-filling phrase, the "aristocracy of letters." The survival of the fittest is as good in the evolution of our literature as of our bodies, and the best "academy" for the writers of the United States is, after all, and in the last analysis, to be found in the judgment of the people, exercised throughout the lapse of a considerable time. For, give the people time enough, and they will always decide justly.

It was in connection with this talk about an "Academy" that Mr. Hall Caine has made the remark that "no academic study of a thing so variable, emotional and independent as the imaginative writer's art could be anything but mischievous." One is inclined to take exception to the statement. Why should the academic study of the principles of writing fiction be mischievous? Is it not possible to codify in some way the art of *construction* of novels so that they may be studied to advantage? This has, of course, never been done. But one believes that, if managed carefully and with a

proper disregard of "set forms" and hampering
conventions, it would be possible to start and
maintain a school of fiction-writing in the
most liberal sense of the word "school." Why
should it be any more absurd than the painting
schools and music schools? Is the art of music,
say, any less variable, less emotional, less
independent, less imaginative than the fiction-
writer's. Heretical as the assertion may appear, one is thoroughly convinced that the art
of novel writing (up to a certain point, *bien
entendu*) can be acquired by instruction just as
readily and with results just as satisfactory
and practical as the arts of painting, sculpture,
music, and the like. The art of fiction is, in
general, based upon four qualities of mind:
observation, imagination, invention and sympathy. Certainly the first two are "acquired
characters." Kindergarten children the world
over are acquiring them every day. Invention
is immensely stimulated by observation and
imagination, while sympathy is so universally
a fundamental quality with all sorts and conditions of men and women—especially the latter
—that it needs but little cultivation. Why,
then, would it be impossible for a few of our
older, more seriously minded novelists to
launch a School of Instruction in the Art
of Composition—just as Bougereau, Lefevre,

Boulanger and Tony Robert Fleury founded Julien's in Paris?

At present the stimulus to, and even the manner of, production of very much of American fiction is in the hands of the publishers. No one not intimately associated with any one of the larger, more important "houses" can have any idea of the influence of the publisher upon latter-day fiction. More novels are written—practically—to order than the public has any notion of. The publisher again and again picks out the man (one speaks, of course, of the younger generation), suggests the theme, and exercises, in a sense, all the functions of instructor during the period of composition. In the matter of this "picking out of the man" it is rather curious to note a very radical change that has come about in the last five years. Time was when the publisher waited for the unknown writer to come to him with his manuscript. But of late the Unknown has so frequently developed, under exploitation and by direct solicitation of the publisher, into a "money-making proposition" of such formidable proportions that there is hardly a publishing house that does not now hunt him out with all the resources at its command. Certain fields are worked with the thoroughness, almost, of a political canvass, and if a given

State—as, for instance, Indiana—has suddenly evolved into a region of great literary activity, it is open to suspicion that it is not because there is any inherent literary quality in the people of the place greater than in other States, but that certain firms of publishers are "working the ground."

It might not have been altogether out of place if upon the Victor Hugo monument which has just been unveiled in Paris there had been inscribed this, one of the most important of the great Frenchman's maxims:

"Les livres n'ont jamais faites du mal";

and I think that in the last analysis, this is the most fitting answer to Mr. Carnegie, who, in his address before the Author's Club, put himself on record as willing to exclude from the libraries he is founding all books not three years old. No doubt bad books have a bad influence, but bad books are certainly better than no books at all. For one must remember that the worst books are not printed—the really tawdry, really pernicious, really evil books. These are throttled in manuscript by the publishers, who must be in a sense public censors. No book, be assured, goes to press but that there is— oh, hidden away like a grain of mustard— some bit, some modicum, some tiny kernel of

good in it.   Perhaps it is not that seed of goodness that the cultured, the fastidious care much
about.   Perhaps the discriminating would call
it a platitude.   But one is willing to believe
that somewhere, somehow, this atom of real
worth makes itself felt—and that's a beginning.
It will create after awhile a taste for reading.
And a taste for reading is a more important
factor in a nation's literary life than the birth
of a second Shakespeare.

It is the people, after all, who "make a literature."   If they read, the few, the "illuminati,"
will write.   But first must come the demand—
come from the people, the Plain People, the
condemned *bourgeoisie*.   The select circles of
the élite, the "studio" hangers-on, the refined,
will never, never, clamour they never so loudly,
toil they never so painfully, produce the Great
Writer.   The demand which he is to supply
comes from the Plain People—from the masses,
and not from the classes.   There is more significance as to the ultimate excellence of American
letters in the sight of the messenger boy
devouring his "Old Sleuths" and "Deadwood
Dicks" and "Boy Detectives," with an *earnest*,
serious absorption, than in the spectacle of a
"reading circle" of dilletanti coquetting with
Verlaine and *pretending* that they understand.

By the same token, then, is it not better to

welcome and rejoice over this recent "literary deluge" than to decry it? One is not sure it is not a matter for self-gratulation—not a thing to deplore and vilify. The "people" are reading, that is the point; it is *not* the point that immature, untrained writers are flooding the counters with their productions. The more the Plain People read the more they will discriminate. It is inevitable, and by and by they will demand "something better." It is impossible to read a book without formulating an opinion upon it. Even the messenger boy can tell you that, in *his* judgment, No. 3,666, "The James Boys Brought to Bay," is more—or less, as the case may be—exciting than No. 3,667, "The Last of the Fly-by-nights." Well, that is something. Is it not better than that the same boy should be shooting craps around the corner? Take his dime novel from him, put him in the "No Book" condition—and believe me, he will revert to the craps. And so it is higher up the scale. In the name of American literature, let the Plain People read, anything—anything, whether it is three days or three years old. Mr. Carnegie will not educate the public taste by shutting his libraries upon recent fiction. The public taste will educate itself by *much* reading, not by *restricted* reading. "Books have never done harm,"

Victor Hugo said it, and a bad book—that is to say, a poor, cheap, ill-written, "trashy" book—is not after all so harmful as "no book" at all.

Later on, when the people have learned discrimination by much reading, it will not be necessary to bar fiction not three years old from the libraries, for by then the people will demand the "something better," and the writers will have to supply it—or disappear, giving place to those who can, and *then* the literary standards will be raised.

II

In a recent number of his periodical, the editor of *Harper's Weekly* prints a letter received from a gentleman who deplores the fact that the participants in the Harvard-Yale track teams are given a great place in the daily newspapers while—by implication—his son, an arduous student and winner of a "Townsend prize," is completely and definitely ignored. "I could not but think of my son," writes the gentleman, "a Yale Senior who, as one of the results of nine years' devotion to study, won a Townsend prize." One will ask the reader to consider this last statement. The publicity of the college athletes is not the point here. The point is "nine years' devotion to study" and—"a Townsend prize." Nine years —think of it—the best, the most important of a boy's life given to devoted study!—not of Men, not of Life, not of Realities, but of the books of Other People, mere fatuous, unreasoned, pig-headed absorption of ideas at secondhand. And the result? Not a well-ordered mind, not a well-regulated reasoning machine, not a power of appreciation, not an ability to create. None of these, but—Great Heavens !— a *Townsend Prize*, a rectangular piece of the skin of a goat, dried and cured and marked with certain signs and symbols by means of a black pigment; this and a disk of the same metal the Uganda warrior hangs in his ears. A Townsend Prize. And for this a young American living in the twentieth century, sane, intelligent, healthful, has pored over Other People's books, has absorbed Other People's notions, has wearied his brain, has weakened his body, has shut himself from the wide world, has denied himself, has restrained himself, has stultified emotion, has in a word buried his talent in the earth wrapped carefully in a napkin. "And," comments the editor, "the boy who won the Townsend prize for scholarship, if he keeps on, will some day be honoured by his fellowmen, when the athletic prize-winner, if he does nothing else, will be a director of a gymnasium. The serious worker comes out ahead every time." But winning Townsend prizes by nine years of study is, we submit, not serious work, but serious misuse of most valuable time and energy. Scholarship? Will we never learn that times change and that sauce for the Renaissance goose is *not* sauce for the New Century gander? It is a fine thing, this scholarship, no doubt; but if a man be content with merely this his scholarship is of as much use and benefit to his contemporaries as his deftness in manicuring his finger nails. The United States in this year of grace of nineteen hundred and two does not want and does not need Scholars, but Men—Men made in the mould of the Leonard Woods and the Theodore Roosevelts, Men such as Colonel Waring, Men such as Booker Washington. The most brilliant scholarship attainable by human effort is not, to-day, worth nine years of any young man's life. I think it is Nathaniel Hawthorne who tells the story of a "scholar" who one day, when a young man, found the tooth of a mammoth. He was a student of fossil remains, and in his enthusiasm set out to complete the skeleton. His mind filled with this one idea, to the exclusion of all else, he traveled up and down the world, year after year, picking up here a vertebra, here a femur, here a rib, here a clavicle. Years passed; he came to be an old man; at last he faced death. He had succeeded. The monstrous framework was complete. But he looked back upon the sixty years of his toil and saw that it was a vanity. He had to show for his life-work—the skeleton of a mammoth. And, believe this implicitly: if—as the editor and commentator remarks—if the Townsend prize-winner *keeps on*, this will be the result, a huge thing no doubt, a thing that looms big in the eye and in the imagination, but an empty thing, lifeless, bloodless, dead; yes and more than dead—extinct; a mere accumulation of dry bones, propped up lest it fall to the ground, a thing for the wind to blow through and the vulgar to gape at.

But in connection with this subject one may cite so high an authority as Doctor Patton of Princeton, who has recently said that nowadays men do not go to colleges to become scholars, and that it was time and money wasted to try to make them such. This is a good saying and should be taken to heart by every college faculty between the oceans. Sooner or later there is bound to come a fundamental change in the mode of instruction now in favour in most American colleges. The times demand it; the character of the student body, the character of the undergraduate, is changing. One chooses to believe that the college of the end of the present century will be an institution where only specialized work will be indulged in. There will be courses in engineering, in electricity, in agriculture, in law, in chemistry, in biology, in mining, etc., and the so-called general "literary" or "classical" courses will be relegated to the limbo of Things

No Longer Useful. Any instructor in collegiate work will tell you to-day that the men in the special courses are almost invariably the hardest, steadiest, most serious workers. The man who studies law at college finishes his work a lawyer, he who studies engineering ends an engineer, the student of biology graduates a biologist, the student of chemistry, a chemist. But the student in the "literary" course does not—no, not once in a thousand instances—graduate a literary man. He spends the four years of his life over a little Greek, a little Latin, a little mathematics, a little literature, a little history, a little "theme" writing, and comes out—just what it would be difficult to say. But he has in most cases acquired a very pronounced distaste for the authors whose work he has studied in class and lecture-room. Great names such as those of Carlyle, Macaulay and De Quincey are associated in his mind only with tedium. He never will go back to these books, never read with enjoyment what once was "work." Even his conscientiousness—supposing him to be animated with such a motive—will trap him and trick him. I do not think that I shall ever forget the spectacle and impression of a student in my own Alma Mater—a little lass of seventeen (the college was co-educational), with her hair still down her back and her shoes yet innocent of heels, rising in her place in the classroom to read before a half-hundred of raw boys and undeveloped girls—not three months out of the high school—a solemn and quite unintelligible "theme" on "The Insincerity of Thomas Babington Macaulay."

Just at the time of the present writing a controversy has been started in London literary circles as to the legitimacy of a reviewer publishing the whole or parts of the same unsigned article in two or more periodicals. Mr. Arthur Symons is the reviewer under fire, and his article a *critique* of the dramas of Mr. Stephen Phillips. It was Mr. Phillips, so we are told, who first started the protest, and he has found followers and champions. And on first consideration there does seem to be ground for complaint here. It has been assumed that the first publisher of the article has a right to expect that for the money he pays to the writer this latter shall give to him all he has to say upon the subject. If he has very much to say— enough for another article—is it not the duty of the scribe to condense and compact so that the matter may be represented as a unit and not as a fragment? Moreover, does it seem fair to Mr. Phillips that three reviews—as was the case—all unfavourable, should appear in as many publications, thus giving to the public the impression that a *group* of critics, instead of merely one, was hostile to his work? Lastly, it has been urged that it is not honest to sell a thing twice—that if a horse has been sold by A to B, A cannot sell it again to C.

But none of the objections seems valid. If the space allotted to the article in the paper is not sufficient, that is the fault of the editor, not the writer. The editor pays only for what he prints: the surplusage is still the author's property and can be by him disposed of as such. As tor the public considering the single—unfavourable—review as the opinions of three men, and as such unfair to Mr. Phillips, this as well is inadequate and incompetent. Another critic, reviewing Mr. Phillips *favourably*, is just as much at liberty to split up his work as the adverse reviewer. Last of all, it *is* under certain circumstances perfectly honest to sell the same thing twice. Articles, stories, poems and the like are continually syndicated in hundreds of newspapers simultaneously, and in this sense are sold over and over again. The analogy between the sale of a horse and the sale of a bit of literature is quite misleading. For the matter of that, the writer does not sell the actual concrete *manuscript* of his work, but merely the right to print it, and unless the word "exclusively" is understood in the agreement he is in no wise bound. The writer is not selling his copy as the owner sells his horse. The analogy would be true if A sold to B the *use* of the horse. When B had got the "use" out of the animal no one will deny the right of A to sell the same "use" to C, D, E, and so on through the whole alphabet. The reviewer of books has a hard enough time of it as it is. It is only fair to give him the same freedom as a livery stable keeper.

It has often occurred to me as a thing of some importance and certain significance that all great travelers are great writers. And the fact is so well established, the effect flows so nvariably from the cause, that there would seem to be here a matter for reflection. One affirms and will maintain that the one is the direct result of the other, that the faculty of adequate expression, of vivid presentation, of forceful and harmonious grouping of words, is engendered and stimulated and perfected by wide journeying.

This is not at all an orthodox view, not at all the theory cherished by our forbears. The writer, according to unvarying belief, is the man of the closet, the bookish man, a student, a sedentary, a consumer of kerosene, a reader rather than a rover. And the idea is plausible.

The nomad, he without local habitation, has no leisure, no opportunity, nor even actual concrete place to write. Would it not seem that literature is the quiet art, demanding an unperturbed mind, an unexcited, calm, reposeful temperament? This is a very defensible position, but it is based upon a foundation of sand. It assumes that the brain of the writer is a jar full of a precious fluid—a bottle full of wine to be poured out with care and with a hand so quiet, so restful and unshaken that not a drop be spilled. Very well. But when the jar, when the bottle is emptied—then what? Believe me, the gods give but one vintage to one man. There will be no refilling of the vessel; and even the lees are very flat, be the wine ever so good. The better the grape, the bitterer the dregs; and the outpouring of the "best that is in you" in the end will be soured by that brackish, *fade* sediment that follows upon lavish expenditure, so that the man ends ignobly and because of exhaustion and depletion, with all the product of his early and mature richness making more prominent and pitiful the final poverty and tenuity of his outgiving—ends the butt of critics, the compassion of the incompetent, a shard kicked of every scullion.

And in all the world there is nothing more lamentable than this—the end of a man once

strong who has used himself up but who decants
lees and not wine. Even when the lees are
spent he absorbs them once more and once
more gives them forth, each time a little staler,
a little thinner, a little feebler, realizing his
exhaustion, yet—urged by some whip of fortune—forced to continue the miserable per-
formance till the golden bowl be broken and
the pitcher shattered at the fountain.

But suppose the productive power of the
writer be considered not as a golden bowl to
be emptied and in the end broken, but as a
silver cord of finest temper that only needs to be
kept in tune.   True, the cord may be stretched
to the breaking-point.   But its end comes at
the very height and in the very consummate
fulness of its capacity, and oh, the grand world-
girdling Note that it sends forth in the breaking!
—the very soul of it at mightiest tension, the
very spirit of it at fiercest strain.   What matter
the loosening or the snapping when so noble
an *Amen* as that vibrates through the nations
to sound at once the Height and the End of
an entire Life—a whole existence concentrated
into a single cry!

Or it may become out of tune. But this is
no great matter, because so easily remedied.
The golden bowl once emptied there will be
no refilling, but by some blessed provision of

heaven nothing is easier than to attune the cords of being which are also the cords—the silver singing cords—of expression.

But—and here we come around once more to the *point de depart*—the silver cords once gone *dis*cordant, once jaded and slack, will not, cannot be brought again to harmony in the closet, in the study, in the seclusion of the cabinet. Tinker them never so cunningly, never so delicately, they will *not* ring true for you. Thought will avail nothing, nor even rest, nor even relaxation. Of oneself, one cannot cause the Master-note to which they will respond to vibrate. The cords have been played on too much. For all your pottering they will yet remain a little loose, and so long as they are loose the deftest fingering, the most skilful touch, will produce only false music.

And the deadly peril is that the cords of Life and the cords of expression lie so close together, are so intricately mingled, that the man cannot always tell that the cords of expression are singing out of tune. Life and expression are two parts of the same instrument. If the whole life be out of tune, how can the man distinguish the false music from the true? There is a danger here, but it is not great. Sooner or later the conviction comes that the productive power is menaced. A little frankness with oneself, a little uncompromising testing of the strings, and the dissonance begins to impress itself.

And—as was said—the remedy is not to be found by the taking of thought, but by an heroic, drastic thrusting out from the grooves and cogs of the life of other men—of the life of the city and the comfortable stay-at-home, hour-to-hour humdrum, and a determined journeying out into the great wide world itself.

The further a-field the better. The Master-note will not be heard within "commuting distance of the city." The whir of civilization smothers it. The click of the telegraph, the hiss of steam and the clatter of the printing-press drown it out. It is not always and of necessity a loud note. Though Nansen heard it in the thunder of the pack-ice of the Farthest North, it came to the ear of Stevenson in the lap of lazy wavelets in the hushed noonday of a South Sea strand.

Travel is the only way. Travel in any direction, by any means, so only it be far— very, very far—is the great attuner of the list-less cords of the writer's instrument. For again and again and again his power is *not* a bowl to be emptied, but an instrument to be played on. To be of use it *must* be sensitive and responsive and true. And to be kept sensi-

tive and responsive and true it must go once
in so often to the great Tuner—to Nature.

We speak of the Mountains, the Rivers,
Deserts and Oceans as though we knew them.
We know the Adirondacks from a fortnight in a
"summer camp"; the Rivers and the Deserts
in kinetoscopic glimpses from the Pullman's
windows; the Ocean—God forgive us!—from
the beach of a "resort" or the deck of an
Atlantic "greyhound." And I think the gods
of the Mountains, Rivers, Deserts and Oceans
must laugh in vast contempt of our credulity
to suppose that we have found their secrets or
heard their music in this timid, furtive peeping
and pilfering. For such little minds as these
the gods have inexhaustible stores of tinkling
cymbals and sounding brasses—Brummagem
ware that they sell us for the price of "commu-
tation tickets" and mileage-books.

The real knowledge, the real experience that
tautens and trims the fibers of being, that tunes
the cords, is a very different matter. The trail
and the tall ship lead to those places where the
Master-note sounds, lead to those untracked,
uncharted corners of the earth, and dull indeed
must be the tympanum that once within ear-
shot cannot hear its majestic diapason. It
sounds in the canyons of the higher mountains,
in the plunge of streams and swirling of rivers

yet without names—in the wildernesses, the plains, the wide-rimmed deserts. It sings a sonorous rhapsody in the rigging of the clipper ship driven by the trade winds, in the ratlines and halyards of South Sea schooners, and drums "reveille" on the tense, hard sails of the fishing-boats off the "Banks." You can hear it in the cry of the lynx, the chant of the wild goose, the call of the moose, and in the "break" of the salmon in the deeper pools below the cataract. It is in the roar of the landslide and in the drone of the *cicada;* in the war-whoop of the savage and in the stridulating of crickets; in the thunder of the tempest and in the faintest breath of laziest zephyrs.

And the silver cord of our creative faculty— the thing nearest to perfection in all the make-up of our imperfect human nature—responds to this Master-note with the quickness and sensitiveness of music-mathematics; responds to it, attunes itself to it, vibrates with its vibration, thrills with its quivering, beats with its rhythm, and tautens itself and freshens itself and lives again with its great pure, elemental life, and the man comes back once more to the world of men with a true-beating heart, and a true-hearing ear, so that he understands once more, so that his living, sensitive, delicately humming instrument trembles responsive to the emotions and impulses and loves and joys and sorrows and fears of his fellows, and the Man writes true and clear, and his message rings with harmony and with melody, with power and with passion of the prophets interpreting God's handwriting to the world of men.

III

THERE can be no question nor reasonable doubt that the "language, institutions and religion" of fiction writers are at present undergoing the most radical revolution in the history of literature. And I mean by that that the men themselves are changing—their characters, their attitudes toward life; even the mode and manner of their own life. Those who are not thus changing are decaying. And those others, the Great Unarrived who do not recognize the Change, who do not acknowledge the Revolution, will never succeed, but will perish untimely almost before they can be said to have been born at all.

Time was when the author was an aristocrat, living in seclusion, unspotted from the world. But the Revolution of which there is question here has meted out to him the fate that Revolutions usually prepared for Aristocrats, and his successor is, must be, *must* be—if he is to voice the spirit of the times aright, if he is to interpret his fellows justly—the Man of the People, the Good Citizen.

How the novelists of the preceding generation played the Great Game is no matter for discussion here. Times were different then. One shut oneself in the study; one wore a velvet coat; one read a great deal and quoted Latin; one knew the classics; one kept apart from the vulgar profane and never, never, never read the newspapers. But for the novelist of the next fifty years of this twentieth century these methods, these habits, this conception of literature as a cult, as a refinement to be kept inviolate from the shoulderings and elbowings of the Common People is a clog, is a stumbling-block, is a pitfall, a bog, mire, trap—anything you like that is false, misleading and pernicious.

I have no patience with a theory of literature —and oh, how often one hears it preached!— that claims the Great Man belongs only to the cultured few. "You must write," so these theorists explain, "for that small number of fine minds who because of education, because of delicate, fastidious taste are competent to judge." I tell you this is wrong. It is precisely the same purblind prejudice that condemned the introduction of the printing-press because it would cheapen and vulgarize the literature of the day. A literature that cannot be vulgarized is no literature at all and will perish just as surely as rivers run to the sea. The things that last are the understandable things

—understandable to the common minds, the Plain People, understandable, one is almost tempted to say, to the very children.

It is so in every branch of art: in music, painting, sculpture, architecture. The great monuments of these activities, the things that we retain longest and cherish with the most care are plain almost to bareness. The most rudimentary mind can understand them. All the learning, all the culture, all the refinement in the world will not give you a greater thrill on reading your "Iliad" than the boy of fifteen enjoys. Is the "Marseillaise" a thing of subtlety or refinement? Are the Pyramids complex? Are Angelo's Sibyls involved? But the "Iliad," the "Marseillaise," the Pyramids, the Sibyls will endure and endure and endure while men have eyes to see, ears to hear and hearts to be moved. These great things, these monuments were *not* written nor composed, nor builded, nor painted for the select, for the cultured. When Homer wrote there were no reading circles. Rouget de Lisle gave no "recitals." One does not have to "read up" to understand the message of Cheops, nor take a course of art lectures to feel the mystery of the Delphic Sibyl.

And so to come back to the starting place, the Revolution in the character of the writer of fiction. If the modern novelist does not understand the Plain People, if he does not address himself directly to them intelligibly and simply, he will fail. But he will never understand them by shutting himself away from them. He must be—and here one comes to the conclusion of the whole matter—a Man of the World. None more so. Books have no place in his equipment, have no right to be there; will only cumber and confuse him. His predecessor never read the newspapers, but for him the newspaper is more valuable than all the tomes of Ruskin, all the volumes of Carlyle. And more valuable than all are the actual, vital Affairs of Men. The function of the novelist of this present day is to comment upon life as he sees it. He cannot get away from this; this is his excuse for existence, the only claim he has upon attention. How necessary then for him— of all men—to be in the midst of life! He cannot plunge too deeply into it. Politics will help him, and Religious Controversies, Explorations, Science, the newest theory of Socialism, the latest development of Biology. He should find an interest in Continental diplomacy and should have opinions on the chances of a Russo-Japanese war over the Corean question. He should be able to tell why it is of such unusual importance for Queen Wilhelmina of

Holland to give birth to an heir, and should know who ought to be nominated for Governor of his native State at the next convention.

No piece of information—mere downright acquisition of fact—need be considered worthless. Nothing is too trivial to be neglected. I know a novelist of international reputation who told me that the following little bits of knowledge (collected heaven knows where and stored up for years in some pigeon-hole of his memory) had been of use to him in the composition of a novel he is now at work upon: That great cities tend to grow to the westward; that race-horses are shod with a long and narrow shoe; and that the usual price charged by an electrician for winding an armature is four dollars. And he seemed prouder of the fact that he had these tiny odds and ends at his command, when needed, than he was of the honorary degree just conferred upon him by Harvard University.

I suppose this is an exaggerated case, and it is not to be denied that it is better to have a Harvard degree than to know the shape of a race-horse's shoe, but it surely goes to prove the point that, as far as actual material worth and use were concerned, the fugitive foolish memory-notes were of more present help than the university degree, and that so far as information is concerned the novelist cannot know too much.

In a recent number of *The Bookman* there appears an able article under the title "Attacking the Newspapers." The title is a trifle misleading, since the author's point and text are a defense of modern journalism, or rather let us say an apology. The apology is very well done. The manner of presentation is ingenious, the style amusing, but none the less one cannot let the article pass without protest or, at the least, comment.

The original function of a newspaper was, and still should be, to tell the news—and, if you please, nothing more than that. The "policy" of the paper was (before the days of the yellow press) advocated and exploited in the editorial columns.

The whole difficulty lies in the fact that nowadays the average newspaper is violently partizan and deliberately alters news to suit its partizanship. "Not a very criminal procedure," I hear it said; "for by reading the opposition papers the public gets the other side." But one submits that such a course *is* criminal, and that it can be proved to be such. How many people do you suppose read the "opposition" papers? The American newspaper readers have not time to read "both sides" unless presented to them in one and the same paper.

Observe now how this partizanship works injustice and ruin. Let us suppose a given newspaper is hostile to the Governor of the State. Now every man—even a journalist— has a right to his opinions and his hostilities, and important men in public life must expect to be abused. There are for them compensations; their position is too high, too secure to be shaken by the vituperation of malevolent journals. But these journals have one favourite form of attacking important public men which, though it does not always harm the personage assaulted, may easily ruin the subordinates with which he surrounds himself. This is the habit of discrediting the statesman by defaming his appointees. The Governor, we will say, has appointed John Smith to be the head of a certain institution of the State. But the Governor has incurred the enmity of the *Daily Clarion*—the leading newspaper. Promptly the *Clarion* seizes upon Smith. His career as head of the institution has been a record of misrule (so the *Clarion* reads), has been characterized by extravagance, incompetency, mismanagement, and even misappropriation of the State's money. And here begins the cruel injustice of the business. The editor

of that paper will set no bounds upon the
lengths to which he will urge his reporters in
their vilification of Smith. The editor knows
he is a liar, the reporters know they are liars,
but the public, ninety-nine times out of a
hundred, ignoring motives, unable to see that
the real object of attack is the Governor,
unable to understand the brute callousness and
wretched hypocrisy of the whole proceeding,
believes the calumny, believes that Smith is an
incompetent, a spendthrift, even a thief.
And even the better class of readers, even the
more intelligent who make allowances for the
paper's political prejudices, will listen to the
abuse and believe that there "must be some
fire where there is so much smoke." Do you
suppose for one moment that Smith will ever
get a hearing in that paper? Do you suppose
its reporters will ever credit him with a single
honest achievement, a single sincere effort?
If you do, you do not understand modern
journalism.

Ah, but the opposition papers! They will
defend Smith. They will champion him as
vehemently as the *Clarion* attacks. That is
all very well, but suppose there are no opposition
papers. Politics are very complicated. The
press of a given community is not always
equally divided between the Republican and

Democratic parties. Time and time again it happens that all the leading newspapers of a city, a county, or even a State, Democratic, Republican, Independent, etc., are banded together to oppose some one Large Man.

Where then will Smith get his hearing? He cannot fight all the newspapers at once. He is not strong enough to retaliate even upon the meanest. The papers are afraid of nothing he can do. They hold absolute power over his good name and reputation. And for the sake of feeding fat the grudge they bear the Great One they butcher the subordinate without ruth and without reproach. Believe me, it has been shown repeatedly that, placed in such a position, the modern newspaper will check at no lie however monstrous, at no calumny however vile. If Smith holds a position of trust he will be trumpeted from end to end of the community as a defaulter, gambling away the public moneys entrusted to his care. He will be pictured as a race-track follower, a supporter of fast women, a thief, a blackguard, and a reprobate. If he holds an administrative office, it will be shown how he has given and taken bribes; how he has neglected his duties and ignored his responsibilities till his office has engendered calamity, ruin, and even actual physical suffering.   If his work is in the nature of supervision over one of those State institutions where the helpless are cared for— the infirm, the imbecile, the aged, or sick, or poor—his cruelty to his wards will be the theme, and he will be written of and pictured as whipping or torturing old men and little children, imprisoning, tormenting, making a hell of what was meant to be a help.

And the man once blackened after this fashion will never again rehabilitate himself in the eyes of the public.   The people who read newspapers always believe the worst, and when an entire press, or even the major part of it, unite to defame a man there is no help or redress possible.   He is ruined, ruined professionally and financially, ruined in character, in pocket, and in the hopes of ever getting back the good name that once was his.

And all this is done merely as a political move, merely to discredit the Big Man who put Smith in his place, merely to hurt his chances of renomination, merely to cut down the number of his votes.   It is butchery; there is no other word than this with which to characterize the procedure, butchery as cruel, as wanton and as outrageous as ever bloodied the sands of the Colosseum.   It is even worse than this, for the victim has no chance for his life.   His hands are tied before the beasts are loosed. He is trussed and downed before the cages are opened, and the benches thunder for his life, not as for a victim to be immolated, but as a criminal to be punished. He is getting only his deserts, his very memory is an execration, and his name whenever mentioned is a by-word and a hissing.

And this in face of the fact that the man may be as innocent of the charges urged as if he had never been born.

Yet Doctor Colby in *The Bookman* article writes: "If we must attack the newspapers let it be as critics, not as crusaders, for the people who write for them are under no stricter obligations than ourselves." What! the reporter or the editor who by some fillip of fortune is in a position to make public opinion in the minds of a million people under no more obligations than you and I! If every obligation bore down with an all but intolerable weight it is in just his case. His responsibility is greater than that of the Pulpit, greater than that of the Physician, greater than that of the Educator. If you would see the use to which it is put, you have only to try to get at the real truth in the case of the next public character assailed and vilified in the public prints.

Doctor Colby is wrong. It *is* a crusade and

not a criticism that will put down the modern yellow newspaper from the bad eminence to which the minds of the hysterical, of the violent, of the ignorant, brutal and unscrupulous have exalted it.

IV

THERE is a certain journal of the Middle
West of the United States which has
proclaimed, with a great flourish of trumpets,
that Mme. Humbert of Paris would have made
a great "fictionist" if she had not elected to
become a great swindler. This is that Mme.
Humbert who cheated a number of bankers,
capitalists and judges out of a great deal of
money with a story of $20,000,000 in a safe
which for certain reasons she could not open.
Very naturally, when her hand was forced the
safe was empty. And this person, the Middle
West paper claims, is a great novelist *manquée*,
"a female Dumas or Hugo." The contention
would not be worthy of notice were it not for
the fact that it is an opinion similar to that
held by a great number of people intelligent
enough to know better. In a word, it is the
contention that the personal morality of the
artist (including "fictionists") has nothing
to do with his work, and that a great rascal
may be a good painter, good musician, good
novelist. With painters, musicians and the

like this may or may not be true. With the novelist one contends, believes and avers that it is absolutely and unequivocally false, and that the mind capable of theft, of immorality, of cruelty, of foulness, or falseness of any kind is incapable, under any circumstances, or by any degree of stimulation, of producing one single important, artistic or useful piece of fiction. The better the personal morality of the writer, the better his writings. Tolstoi, for instance: it is wholly and solely due to the man's vast goodness and philanthropy that his novels carry weight. The attitude of the novelist toward his fellow-men and women is the great thing, not his inventiveness, his ingenuity, his deftness, or glibness, or verbal dexterity. And the mind wholly mean, who would rob a friend of $40,000 (after the manner of the Humbert person), or could even wilfully and deliberately mar the pleasure of a little child, could never assume toward the world at large that attitude of sympathy and generosity and toleration that is the first requisite of the really great novelist. Always you will find this thing true: that the best, the greatest writers of fiction are those best loved of troops of friends; and for the reason that, like the Arab philosopher of the poem, they, first of all, have "loved their fellow-men." It is this that

has made their novels great. Consider Stevenson, or our own "Dean," or Hugo, or Scott,
men of the simplest lives, uncompromising in
rectitude, scrupulously, punctiliously, Quixoti-
cally honest; their morality—surely in the cases
of Stevenson and Hugo—setting a new standard
of religion, at the least a new code of ethics.
And thus it goes right down the line, from the
greater lights to the lesser and to the least. It
is only the small men, the "minor" people
among the writers of books who indulge in
eccentricities that are only immortalities under
a different skin; who do not pay their debts;
who borrow without idea of returning; who
live loose, "irregular," wretched, vicious lives,
and call it "Bohemianism," and who believe
that "good work" can issue from the turmoil,
that the honeycomb will be found in the
carcass, and the sweet come forth from the
putrid. So that in the end one may choose to
disagree with the Middle West editor and to
affirm that it is not the ingenious criminal who
is the novelist *manqué*, but the philanthropist,
the great educator, the great pulpit orator, the
great statesman. It is from such stuff that the
important novels are made, not from the
deranged lumber and disordered claptrap of the
brain of a defective.

In the course of a speech made at a recent

dinner given in London, Sir Donald Mackenzie Wallace has deplored the fact that our present generation of English writers has produced no worthy successors to the great men of the mid-Victorian period—that there are no names to place beside Scott, Dickens, Thackeray, Browning, or Keats. But he also brought forward extenuating circumstances, chief among which was the fact that the novelists of to-day were working overtime to supply the demands of an ever-increasing public, and that, by implication, their work was therefore deteriorating. One does not believe that this is so. Rapid work may cause the deterioration of a commercial article, but it by no means follows that the authors who are called upon to produce a very large number of books are forced into the composition of unworthy literature. The writer's brain does *not* hold the material for his books. It is not like a storehouse, from which things may be taken till nothing remains. The writer's material is life itself, inexhaustible and renewed from day to day, and his brain is only the instrument that adapts life to fiction. True, this instrument itself may wear out after awhile, but it usually lasts as long as the man himself, and is good for more work than the unthinking would believe possible. As a matter of fact, the best novelists have, as a rule, been the most prolific, have been those who had to write rapidly and much to satisfy, if not the demands of the public, then at least other more personal demands, none the less insistent. Scott and Dickens were unusually prolific, yet the rapidity with which they accomplished their work did not hurt the quality of the work itself. Balzac and Dumas produced whole libraries of books and yet kept their standards high. As one has urged before, it is the demand of the People that produces the great writer, not *re*duces the quality and fineness of his work. If he has the "divine spark," the breath of the millions will fan rather than extinguish it.

One does not choose to believe that the art of fiction nor the standards of excellence have deteriorated since the day of Scott, Dickens and Thackeray. True, we have no men to equal them as yet, but they are surely coming. Time was, at the end of the seventeenth century, when the dearth of good fiction was even more marked than at present. But one must bear in mind that progress is never along a direct line, but by action and reaction. A period will supervene when a group of geniuses arise, and during the course of their activities the average of excellence is high, great books are produced, and a whole New Literature is launched. Their influence is

profound; the first subschool of imitators follow
good enough men but second-rate.   These in
turn are followed by the third-raters, and these
by the fourth-raters, and no one is found bold
enough to strike out for himself until the bottom is reached.   Then comes the reaction, and
once more the group of giants towers up from
out the mass.   We are probably living through
the era of the fourth-raters just now, and one
believes that we are rather near to the end even
of that.   The imitators of the romantic school
have imitated to ten places decimals and have
diluted and rediluted till they can hardly go
further without producing something actually
and really new.   At any rate, the time is most
propitious for a Man of Iron who can be bent
to no former shape nor diluted to no old-time
essence.   Then will come the day of the New
Literature, and the wind of Life itself will blow
through the dry bones and fustian and sawdust of the Imitation, and the People will all at
once realize how very far afield the fourth-
raters have drawn them and how very different a good novel is from a bad one.

For say what you will, the People, the Plain
People who Read, do appreciate good literature
in the end.   One must keep one's faith in the
People—the Plain People, the Burgesses, the
Grocers—else of all men the artists are most

miserable and their teachings vain. Let us admit and concede that this belief is ever so sorely tried at times. Many thousands of years ago the wisest man of his age declared that "the People imagine a vain thing." Continually they are running away after strange gods; continually they are admiring the fake and neglecting actual worth. But in the end, and at last, they will listen to the true note and discriminate between it and the false. *In the last analysis the People are always right.* Somehow, and after all is said and done, they will prefer Walter Scott to G. P. R. James, Shakspere to Marlowe, Flaubert to Goncourt. Sometimes the preference is long in forming, and during this formative period they have many reversions, and go galloping, in herds of one hundred or one hundred and fifty thousand (swelling the circulations), after false gods. But note this fact: that the fustian and the tinsel and the sawdust are discovered very soon, and, once the discovery made, the sham idol can claim no single devotee.

In other words, it is a comfort to those who take the literature of the Americans—or even of the Anglo-Saxons—seriously to remember, in the long run and the larger view, that a circulation of two hundred, three hundred or four hundred thousand—judging even by this base-

scale of "copies sold"—is not so huge after all.
Consider. A "popular" novel is launched
and sells its half-million. Within a certain
very limited period of time, at most five years,
this sale stops definitely and conclusively.
The People have found out that it is not such a
work of genius after all, and will have no more
of it. But how about the circulation of the
works of the real Masters, Scott and Dickens,
say—to be more concrete, let us speak of
"Ivanhoe" and "David Copperfield"—have
not each of these "sold" more than two hundred
thousand since publication? Is not two hundred million nearer the mark? And they are
still selling. New editions are published every
year. Does not this prove that the People
are discriminating; that they are—after all—
preferring the best literature to the mediocre;
that they are not such a mindless herd after all;
that in the end, in fine, they are always right?
It will not do to decry the American public;
to say that it has no taste, no judgment; that
it "likes to be fooled." It may be led away
for a time by clamorous advertising and the
"barking" of fakirs. But there comes a day
when it will no longer be fooled. A million
dollars' worth of advertising would not today
sell a hundred thousand copies of "Trilby."
But "Ivanhoe" and "Copperfield," without

advertising, without *reclames* for exploitation, are as marketable this very day as a sack of flour or a bag of wheat.

Mr. Metcalfe, in a recent issue of *Life*, has been lamenting the lack of good plays on the American stage during the past season, and surely no one can aver that the distinguished critic is not right. One cannot forbear a wince or two at the thought of what future art historians will say in their accounts of the American drama at the beginning of the twentieth century. Frankly and unreservedly the native American drama is just about as bad as it can be, and every intelligent-minded person is quite willing to say so. The causes are not difficult to trace. Two come to the mind at once, which in themselves alone would account for the degeneracy —*i. e.*, the rage for Vaudeville and the exploitation of the Star. The first has developed in the last ten years, an importation from English music halls. Considered at first as a fad by the better class of theatre-goers, a thing to be countenanced with amused toleration like performing bears and the animal circus, it has been at length boosted and foisted upon the public attention till, like a veritable cancer, it has eaten almost into the very vitals of the Legitimate Comedy (using the word in its technical sense). Continually nowadays one may

see a "specialty"—generally in the form of a
dance—lugged in between the scenes of a
perfectly sober, perfectly sane Comedy of
Manners. The moment any one subordinate
feature of a dramatic action is developed at the
expense of *vraisemblance* and the Probabilities,
and for the sake of amusing the galleries, there is
the first bacillus of decay. Vaudeville is all
very well by itself, and one will even go so far
as to admit that it has its place as much as
an Ibsen problem-play. But it should keep to
that place. It is ludicrously *out* of place in a
comedy—quite as much so as the "Bible
Incident" in Ebsmith would be in a Hoyt farce.
But because the "specialty," because Vaudeville, will "go" with the "gallery" at any time
and at any place, the manager and—the pity
of it!—the author, too, will introduce it whenever the remotest possibility occurs, and by
just so much the tone of the whole drama is
lowered. It has got to such a pass by now,
however, that one ought to be thankful if this
same "tone" is not keyed down to the specialty.

But the exploiting of the Star, it would seem,
is, of all others, the great cause of the mediocrity
of present-day dramatic literature. One has
but to glance at the theatre programmes and
bills to see how matters stand. The name of the
leading lady or leading man is "scare-headed"

so that the swiftest runner cannot fail to see. Even the manager proclaims his patronymic in enormous "caps." But the author!—as often as not *his* name is not discoverable at all. The play is nothing—thus it would seem the managers would have us believe—it is the actress, her speeches, her scenes, her gowns, her personality, that are the all-important essentials. It is notorious how plays are cut, and readjusted, and dislocated to suit the Star. Never mind whether or not the scene is artistic, is vivid, is dramatic. Does the Star get the best of it? If not, write it over. The Star must have all the good lines. If they cannot be built into the Star's part, cut 'em out. The Probabilities, the construction, artistic effect, climax, even good, common, forthright, horse sense, rot 'em! who cares for 'em? Give the Star the lime-light—that's the point.

If the audience is willing to pay its money to see Miss Marlowe, Miss Mannering or Mrs. Carter put through her paces, that's another thing; but let us not expect that good dramas will issue forth from this state of affairs.

Where are the Books for Girls? Adults' books there are and books for boys by the carload, but where is the book for the young girls? Something has already been said about literature for the amiable young

woman, but this, now, is a very different
person. One means the girl of fourteen to
eighteen. The boy passing through this most
trying formative period finds his literature
ready to hand. Boys' books, tales of hunting,
adventure and sport abound. They are good
books, too, sane, "healthy," full of fine spirit
and life. But the girl, where does she read?
Surely the years between fourteen and eighteen
are even more trying to a young girl than to a
boy. She is not an active animal. When the
boy is out-of-doors, pitching curves or "running
the ends," the girl (even yet in the day and age
of "athletics for women") is in the house, and,
as like as not, reading. And reading what, if
you please? The feeblest, thinnest, most
colourless lucubrations that it is given to the
mind of misguided man to conceive or to per-
petuate. It must be this or else the literature
of the adult; and surely the novels written for
mature minds, for men and women who have
some knowledge of the world and powers of
discrimination, are not good reading, in any
sense of the word, for a sixteen-year-old girl in
the formative period of her life.

Besides Alcott, no one has ever written
intelligently for girls. Surely there is a field
here. Surely a Public, untried and unex-
plored, is wailing for its author; nor is it a

public wanting in enthusiasm, loyalty or intelligence.

But for all this great parade and prating of emancipated women it nevertheless remains a fact that the great majority of twentieth-century opinion is virtually Oriental in its conception of the young girl. The world to-day is a world for boys, men and women. Of all humans, the young girl, the sixteen-year-old, is the least important—or, at least, is so deemed. Wanted: a Champion. Wanted: the Discoverer and Poet of the Very Young Girl. Unimportant she may now appear to you, who may yet call her by her first name without fear and without reproach. But remember this, you who believe only in a world of men and boys and women; the Very Young Girl of to-day is the woman of to-morrow, the wife of the day after, and the mother of next week. She only needs to put up her hair and let down her frocks to become a very important person indeed. Meanwhile, she has no literature; meanwhile, *faute de mieux*, she is trying to read Ouida and many other books intended for maturer minds; or, worse than all, she is enfeebling her mind by the very thin gruel purveyed by the mild-mannered gentlemen and ladies who write for the Sunday-school libraries. Here is a bad business; here is a field that needs cultivation.

All very well to tend and train the saplings, the oaks and the vines. The flowers—they have not bloomed vet—are to be thought about, too.

All the more so that the young girl takes a book to heart infinitely more than a boy. The boy—*his* story once read—votes it "bully," takes down his cap, and there's an end. But the average Very Young Girl does not read her story: she lives it, lingers over it, weeps over it, lies awake nights over it. So long as she lives she will never quite forget the books she read when she was sixteen. It is not too much to say that the "favourite" books of a girl at this age become a part of her life. They influence her character more than any of us, I imagine, would suspect or admit. All the more reason, then, that there should not only be good books for girls, but plenty of good books.

THE END.

BIBLIOGRAPHY, ESSAYS, ARTICLES, LETTERS

"Ancient Armour" (first published article), San Francisco *Chronicle*, March 31, 1889.

Series of letters from South Africa concerning Uitlander Insurrection, published in the San Francisco *Chronicle:* "A Californian in City of Cape Town," January 19, 1896; "In the Compound of a Diamond Mine," February 2, 1896; "From Cape Town to Kimberley Mine," January 26, 1896; "In the Veldt of the Transvaal," February 9, 1896; "A Zulu War Dance," March 15, 1896.

"Types of Western ·Men," published in San Francisco *Wave*, May 2, 1896.

"Western City Types," published in San Francisco *Wave*, May 9, 1896.

"The Bivalve at Home," published in San Francisco *Wave*, July 16, 1896.

"Italy in California," published in San Francisco *Wave*, October 24, 1896.

"A Question of Ideals," published in San Francisco *Wave*, December 26, 1897.

" New Year's at San Quentin," published in San Francisco *Wave*, January 9, 1897.

"Hunting Human Game," published in San Francisco *Wave*, January 23, 1897.

"Passing of Little Pete," published in San Francisco *Wave*, January 30, 1897.

"A California Artist," published in San Francisco *Wave*, February 6, 1897.

"A Lag's Release," published in San Francisco *Wave*, March 12, 1897.

"Among the Cliff-Dwellers," published in San Francisco *Wave*, May 15, 1897.

"The Sailing of the 'Excelsior,'" published in San Francisco *Wave*, July 31, 1897.

"The Tale and the Truth," published in San Francisco *Wave*, September 25, 1897.

"Art Education in San Francisco," published in San Francisco *Wave*, September 25, 1897.

"The End of the Act," published in San Francisco *Wave*, November 27, 1897.

"Comida," published in *Atlantic Monthly*, March, 1899.

"With Lawton to Caney," published in *Century Magazine*, June, 1899.

"Student Life in Paris," published in *Collier's Weekly*, May 12, 1900.

Series of New York letters to *Chicago American*, commencing May, 1901—September, 1901.

Series of Articles to *Boston Transcript*, commencing November 15—February 5 (weekly articles).

"The Unknown Author and the Publisher," published in *World's Work*, April, 1901.

"True Reward of the Novelist," published in *World's Work*, September, 1901.

"Mr. Kipling's 'Kim,'" published in *World's Work*, September, 1901.

"Story-Teller *vs.* Novelist," published in *World's Work*, March, 1902.

"The Frontier Gone at Last," published in *World's Work*, February, 1902.

"The Need of a Literary Conscience," published in *World's Work*, May, 1902.

"The Novel with a Purpose," published in *World's Work*, May, 1902.

Series of articles to *The Critic*, entitled "Salt and Sincerity," published monthly from May to October, 1902.

"Life in the Mining Region," published in *Everybody's Magazine*, September, 1902.

"In Defense of Doctor W. Lawlor," published in San Francisco *Argonaut*, August 11, 1902.

"The Responsibilities of a Novelist," published in *The Critic*, December, 1902.

"The Neglected Epic," published in *World's Work*, December, 1902.

The "Great American Novelist," syndicated, January 19, 1903.

"The American Public and Popular Fiction," syndicated, February 2, 1903.

"Child Stories for Adults," syndicated, February 9, 1903.

"The Nature Revival in Literature," syndicated, February 16, 1903.

"Novelists to Order—While You Wait," syndicated, February 23, 1903.

"Newspaper Criticism and American Fiction," syndicated, March 9, 1903.

"Richard Harding Davis," syndicated, January 26, 1903.

"Chances of Unknown Writers," syndicated, March 2, 1903.

SHORT STORIES

"Babazzouin," published in San Francisco *Argonaut*, May, 1891.

"Son of a Sheik," published in San Francisco *Argonaut*, June, 1891.

"Le Gongleur de Taillebois," published in San Francisco *Wave*, December 25, 1891.

"Arachne," published in San Francisco *Wave*, 1892.

"Lauth," published in *Overland Monthly*, March, 1893.

"Travis Hallets, Half-Back," published in *Overland Monthly*, January, 1894.

"Outward and Visible Signs Series" of short stories, published in the *Overland Monthly*, commencing February, 1894—titles as follows: "Thoroughbred," February, 1894; "She and the Other Fellow," March, 1894; "The Most Noble Conquest of Man," May, 1894; "Outside the Zewana," July, 1894; "After Strange Gods," October, 1894.

"The Caged Lion," published in San Francisco *Argonaut*, August, 1894.

"A Defense of the Flag," published in San Francisco *Argonaut*, October, 1895.

"A Salvation Boom in Matabeleland," published in San Francisco *Wave*, April 25, 1896.

"The Heroism of Jonesie," published in San Francisco *Wave*, May 16, 1896.

Series of Sketches entitled "Man Proposes," published in San Francisco *Wave*, May 23, 1896; May 30, 1896; June 13, 1896; June 27, 1896; July 4, 1896.

"In the Heat of Battle," published in San Francisco *Wave*, December 19, 1896.

"His Sister," published in San Francisco *Wave*, December 28, 1896.

"The Puppets and the Puppy," San Francisco *Wave*, May 22, 1897.

"Beer and Skittles," published in San Francisco *Wave*, May 29, 1897.

"Through a Glass Darkly," published in San Francisco *Wave*, June 12, 1897.

"Little Dramas of the Curbstone," published in San Francisco *Wave*, June 26, 1897.

"The Strangest Thing," published in San Francisco *Wave*, July 3, 1897.

"This Animal of a Buldy Jones," published in San Francisco *Wave*, July 17, 1897.

"Boom," published in San Francisco *Wave*, August 7, 1897.

"Reversion to Type," published in San Francisco *Wave*, August 14, 1897.

"House with the Blinds," published in San Francisco *Wave*, August 21, 1897.

"The Third Circle," published in San Francisco *Wave*, August 28, 1897.

"The End of the Beginning," published in San Francisco *Wave*, September 4, 1897.

"A Case for Lombroso," published in San Francisco *Wave*, September 11, 1897.

"His Single Blessedness," published in San Francisco *Wave*, September 18, 1897.

"Execution without Judgment," published in San Francisco *Wave*, October 2, 1897.

"Miracle Joyeux," published in San Francisco *Wave*, October 9, 1897.

"Judy's Service of Gold Plate," published in San Francisco *Wave*, October 16, 1897.

"The Associated Un-Charities," published in San Francisco *Wave*, October 30, 1897.

"Fantasie Printaniere," published in San Francisco *Wave*, November 6, 1897.

"His Dead Mother's Portrait," published in San Francisco *Wave*, November 13, 1897.

"Shorty Stack, Pugilist," published in San Francisco *Wave*, November 20, 1897.

"Isabella Regina," published in San Francisco *Wave*, November 27, 1897.

"Perverted Tales" (Parodies on several well-known authors), published in San Francisco *Wave*, December 25, 1897: "The Rickshaw that Happened," by R—d K—g; "The Green Stone of Unrest," by S—n Cr—e; "Van Bubble's Story," by R—d H—g D—s; "Ambrosia Beer," by A—e B—e; "I Call on Lady Dotty," by A—y H—e; "The Hero of Tomato Can," by B—t H—e.

"The Drowned Who Do Not Die," published in San Francisco *Wave*, September 24, 1898.

"Miracle Joyeux," republished *McClure's Magazine*, December, 1898.

"This Animal of a Buldy Jones," republished in *McClure's Magazine*, March, 1899.

"The Riding of Felipe," published in *Everybody's Magazine*, March, 1901.

"Buldy Jones, Chef du Claque," published in *Everybody's Magazine*, May, 1901.

"Kirkland at Quarter," published in *Saturday Evening Post*, December 12, 1901.

"A Memorandum of Sudden Death," published in *Collier's Weekly*, January, 1902.

"A Bargain with Peg-leg," published in` *Collier's Weekly*, March 1, 1902.

"Grettir at Drangey," published in *Everybody's Magazine* March, 1902.

"A Statue in an Old Garden," published by *Ladies' Home Journal* about April, 1902.

"Dying Fires," published in *Smart Set* about April, 1902.

"The Passing of Cock-Eye Blacklock," published in *Century Magazine*, July, 1902.

"The Guest of Honour," published in the *Pilgrim Magazine*, July and August, 1902.

" A Deal in Wheat," published in *Everybody's Magazine*, August, 1902.

"Two Hearts That Beat as One," published in *Brander Magazine* (unable to ascertain date).

"The Dual Personality of Slick Dick Nickerson," published in *Collier's Weekly*, November, 1902.

"The Ship That Saw a Ghost," published in *Overland Monthly*, December, 1902.

"The Wife of Chino," published in *Century Magazine*, January, 1903.

"The Ghost in the Cross-Trees," published in New York *Herald*, March, 1903.

POEMS PUBLISHED

"Poitier," medieval ballad, published in *Berklyian Magazine*, 1891.

" Brunhilda," poem, illustrated by author, published in *California Illustrated Magazine* (discontinued), 1891.

"Crepusculum," sonnet, published by *Overland Monthly*, April, 1892.

BOOKS PUBLISHED

"Yvernelle," long poem, published by Lippincott & Company, 1892.

" Moran of the Lady Letty," serialized in San Francisco

Bibliography 311

Wave about January, 1898. Published by Doubleday & McClure, September, 1898.

"McTeague," published by Doubleday & McClure, February, 1899.

"Blix," serialized in *The Puritan* about April, 1899. Published by Doubleday & McClure, September, 1899.

"A Man's Woman," serialized in New York *Evening Sun* about July—October, 1899; in San Francisco *Chronicle*, July 23, 1899—October 8, 1899. Published by Doubleday & McClure, February, 1900.

"Octopus," published by Doubleday, Page & Company, April, 1901.

"The Pit," serialized in *Saturday Evening Post*, September 27, 1902—January 31, 1903. Published by Doubleday, Page & Company, January, 1903.